What people are saying about …

Young and in Love

"*Young and in Love* is a wake-up call for every generation to honor marriage. This book will inspire you to get married, stay married, and enjoy life together. If you have been raised to fear love or marriage, then read this book for a whole new picture of what marriage should be."

Dr. Gary Smalley, best-selling author and speaker

"The most important decision you will make apart from your relationship with God is who you marry. I love Ted Cunningham's passion for marriage and making sure that young people are choosing to marry—but also choosing wisely. He is an emerging and strong voice encouraging the church to fight for marriage in the next generation."

Dr. Tim Clinton, president of the American Association of Christian Counselors

"This isn't just a book; it's a provocation. Cunningham's words are an atom bomb to the popular social moorings that might be accepted, but might not be biblical. Every twentysomething I know should read this book."

Johnnie Moore, vice president and campus pastor of Liberty University and author of *Honestly: Really Living What We Say We Believe*

"Ted Cunningham is one of the most gifted communicators in America. He speaks straight to the heart and straight from the heart. He is brilliant, scriptural, and lots of fun! This book will be one of the best experiences of your life."

Joe White, president of Kanakuk Kamps, author
of more than twenty books, and national speaker

"If you mentor, counsel, or pastor young people today, you need to read *Young and in Love*. It will challenge the cultural lenses through which you have viewed marriage and help you lead singles to learn the value and benefit of commitment. Ted Cunningham is funny and very engaging, but he is serious about restoring marriage in the millennial generation."

Joshua Straub, PhD, American
Association of Christian Counselors,
and coauthor of *God Attachment*

"In *Young and in Love,* Ted Cunningham strips away the myth of a God who hates sex, finds it dirty, and considers it unnatural, and he reintroduces the reader to a divine plan with very personal connections. Ted's message is informative, entertaining, and engaging, and it will not only change your mind about intimacy, it will frame the picture of how love and marriage truly become one."

Shane Stanford, senior pastor of Gulf
Breeze UMC and author of *A Positive Life*
and *The Seven Next Words of Christ*

"If you've ever seen Ted Cunningham speak, you know he's a gifted communicator who will make you think, laugh, and love God more deeply. His new book will challenge you and reignite your passion for marriage."

Margaret Feinberg, author of *Scouting the Divine* and *The Sacred Echo,* www.margaretfeinberg.com

"Ted Cunningham's gift of humor, wisdom, and practical teaching gives us a wonderful guide to create a culture of marriage and lead young lovers into the bliss of marriage. *Young and in Love* is a must-read for young adults, for those who lead these groups, and for anyone who is married or longs to be."

Rev. R. Scott Weatherford, lead pastor of First Alliance Church in Alberta, Canada

"For those truly in love and meeting the biblical and practical criteria for finding a great mate, Pastor Cunningham will help them move ahead as God intended. I really hope that pastors and counselors will integrate Pastor Ted's insights, so the phenomenon of unnecessary prolonged adolescence can be reversed."

Lesley Hurst, program director and host of "Vocal Point" on GraceFM Radio Network and pastor's wife

"I intend to have my premarital mentors read this book so they can incorporate some of this information in their mentoring process. It would be a great gift for any single person or seriously dating or engaged couple."

Sandy Bolen, director of marriage ministry
at Savannah Christian Church

"This book is packed with simple and profound principles that when applied offer a foundation for a forever marriage. Ted's passion for the family comes through in every chapter, and his gift for application to real life is undeniable."

Dr. Alex Himaya, founding pastor
of The Church at BattleCreek

"This book is hands down one of the most compelling and practical arguments I've read for getting to marriage in a timely yet responsible way. Get ready to shatter your assumptions about marrying young, and expect to be called out by Ted if you're standing in the way of a good match. *Young and in Love* will make champions of marriage cheer."

Lisa Anderson, Focus on the Family's
director of young adults and host of
The Boundless Show, www.boundless.org

Young and in Love

Challenging the Unnecessary Delay of Marriage

Ted Cunningham

David C Cook®
transforming lives together

YOUNG AND IN LOVE
Published by David C Cook
4050 Lee Vance View
Colorado Springs, CO 80918 U.S.A.

David C Cook Distribution Canada
55 Woodslee Avenue, Paris, Ontario, Canada N3L 3E5

David C Cook U.K., Kingsway Communications
Eastbourne, East Sussex BN23 6NT, England

The graphic circle C logo is a registered trademark of David C Cook.

The Web site addresses recommended throughout this book are offered as a
resource to you. These Web sites are not intended in any way to be or imply an
endorsement on the part of David C Cook, nor do we vouch for their content.

Unless otherwise noted, all Scripture quotations are taken from the Holy Bible,
New International Version®, NIV™. Copyright © 1973, 1978, 1984 by Biblica,
Inc™. Used by permission of Zondervan. All rights reserved worldwide. www.
zondervan.com. Scripture quotations marked NLT are taken from the New
Living Translation of the Holy Bible. New Living Translation copyright ©
1996, 2004 by Tyndale Charitable Trust. Used by permission of Tyndale House
Publishers. Scripture quotations marked GNT are taken from the Good News
Translation—Second Edition. © 1992 by American Bible Society. Used by
permission. Scripture quotations marked NASB are taken from the *New American
Standard Bible*, © Copyright 1960, 1995 by The Lockman Foundation. Used
by permission. Scripture quotations marked ESV are taken from *The Holy Bible,
English Standard Version*. Copyright © 2000; 2001 by Crossway Bibles, a
division of Good News Publishers. Used by permission. All rights reserved.

LCCN 2011923887
ISBN 978-0-7814-0447-1
eISBN 978-0-7814-0689-5

© 2011 Ted Cunningham
The Team: Alex Field, Sarah Schultz, Caitlyn York, Karen Athen
Cover Design: Amy Kiechlin Konyndyk
Cover Images: iStockphoto, 8240870; 1244186, royalty-free

Printed in the United States of America

First Edition 2011

3 4 5 6 7 8 9 10

051311

To my children,
Corynn and Carson,
and their future spouses

Acknowledgments

I am so grateful to the team at David C Cook. Thank you for believing in this message. Alex Field is a great friend and wordsmith. Thank you to Don Pape, Terry Behimer, Ingrid Beck, Caitlyn York, and the sales and marketing teams for their expertise. This book sparked many spirited conversations at Cook, so thank you for agreeing to put this message into print.

God has blessed me with many tremendous friends and mentors in ministry. Gary Smalley has been a constant encourager and mentor for ten years now. Thank you, Gary, for picturing a special future for me. Joe White shakes his head at me a lot but believes in his pastor. Thank you, Joe, for trusting me to share with Men at the Cross. Margaret Feinberg has been a gracious writing mentor. I PROMISED her that I will never again use all caps in my writing. She hates being yelled at. Michael and Ali Hall, Steve and Barbara Uhlmann, Marc and Jennifer Harris, and Mark and Kay Connelly are all promarriage and have been fantastic partners in ministry.

My dad taught me responsibility before privilege. My mom has been my editor since the fifth grade. I still remember calling home at age twenty-one and telling them about Amy. They were more than enthusiastic. I appreciate my parents' belief in young marriage.

Thank you to my wife, Amy, the first reader of every manuscript. She is brutally honest. She critiques both my writing and speaking. When something needs to be changed, she gently encourages me. I am glad we married early.

My children, Carson and Corynn, find their way into every book. They are getting older and have started reading. I will have to adjust.

Woodland Hills Family Church has always supported my passion in fighting for marriage and family. Angela Jennings is the most passionate Mosaic voice on our staff and edited this book thoroughly. Pam Strayer is a dependable early reader. Jim Sedlacek, Ted Burden, and Denise Bevins run the show while I am studying and writing. Brenda Pannell and Stephanie Watson are always enthusiastic to "take the hit" on my behalf.

Thank you to Herschend Family Entertainment Corporation for allowing us to rent the purple castle for our church family. The Herschend family has always fought for the family, and we are grateful to them.

Contents

Chapter 1

Chase the Foxes

Catch for us the foxes,
the little foxes that ruin the vineyards,
our vineyards that are in bloom.

—Song of Songs 2:15

I am a promarriage pastor. I believe God created marriage to be enjoyed between a man and woman for a lifetime. The only part of creation that God declared as "not good" was man's singleness, and throughout Scripture marriage is normative, while singleness is the exception. So young men need to start approaching young women, falling in love, and getting married—*it's biblical*. I believe Satan has duped our culture into believing the lie that says, "Marriage is the problem, not man." He has convinced us that one of the best ways to prosper in life is to abstain from marriage or at least delay it as long as possible.

Young people have fallen for the lie. Delay marriage, be independent, finish college, build your career, save up your money, and have
sex outside of marriage. You've been told to wait until you have it all
figured out and have found someone who has done the same. That's
why you keep hearing the words, "You're too young."

I believe that young age is an unnecessary delay of marriage. If
you and your fiancé(e) walked into our church today, with budding
love in your hearts, we would rejoice with you, even if you were only
twenty years old. We would walk you through biblical qualifications
for marriage, and if you were ready, we'd give you the pastoral nod.
Then we would set a date and throw a raging party.

Once upon a time, a single Shullamite woman desired the love
of a shepherd king. Her desire was intensely sexual when she shared,

> Let him kiss me with the kisses of his mouth—
>   for your love is more delightful than wine.
> Pleasing is the fragrance of your perfumes;
>   your name is like perfume poured out.
> No wonder the maidens love you!
> Take me away with you—let us hurry!
>   Let the king bring me into his chambers. (Song
>   1:2–4)

Have you experienced such love, and if so, how old were you?
Do you have an intense desire to be with that person forever? Do
you feel God could be knitting the two of you together? Now, have
you ever been invalidated in that love by a friend or family mem-
ber? Has anyone ever told you, "You'll get over it," "There are lots

of options," "You don't know what you need," or "There's time for that later"?

I want to validate your love, help you discern whether God is knitting your hearts together, and then encourage you not to let age stop you. If your parents are listening in, I hope they hear my challenge to you. Remember, you are called to honor Mom and Dad. They in turn must guard their hearts from becoming foxes and destroying the buds of your young love. Solomon pictured young marriage as a blossoming vineyard (Song 2:15). There are many foxes that seek to destroy the bud before it can bloom. Some foxes are intentional, and some are not. Some are vicious, while some are simply misinformed.

My daughter, Corynn, is seven years old, and she is my princess. I write this book to give myself plenty of time to prepare her, her mom, and her future husband. But I do not want to be an overreacting, overprotective parent. Today we use the terms *hovering* and *helicopter* to describe parents who give their children no room to breathe, suppressing their emotions. One day, years from now, Corynn will come home and tell me she has met the man she will marry. At that moment, my plan is to pause, take a breath, load a small firearm, and praise what God may be forming in them.

Last year Corynn started kindergarten. The best part of my day was dropping her off at school each morning at eight thirty. The second best part of my day was picking her up from school in the afternoon. I'll never forget the day she told me about a little boy we'll call "Jason."

"He likes me, Dad," she said.

"Really?" I asked.

"Yep, and I think I like him," she said with one eye closed and head slightly tilted, waiting for my response.

I'd prepared for this day. I told myself I would validate her and not overreact. Too many parents freak out at the signs of young love, and I was not going to be one of them. I would avoid statements like "You're too young!" "What! You don't need to have a boyfriend at this age!" "You can't like him!" or "Boys are evil!"

What we're thinking and want to say is, "I wish you didn't have these feelings at such an early age," "Stop feeling that way," or "You'll get over it and I hope pretty quick!" I rebuke all of those responses in the name of Jesus. Send them back to the pit where they belong!

Corynn was not prepared for my response.

"Well, honey, do you think he is *the one?*" I asked her.

"DAD!" was her reply.

I was prepared to go further. Inspired by my friend Greg Smalley, I was ready to help her work on her first family budget and start looking for their first place. Greg allowed his elementary-school-aged daughter to go so far as to plan where she and her boyfriend would live after they wed, how they would make a living, and even set the date of the wedding. But once they crunched the numbers, it did not seem feasible. He's a great dad.

I'm sure you have a young-love story. It may be the story you are writing at this very moment. You may be asking, "Have I found the right one?" "How long should we date before talking marriage?" "Will my parents approve?" "What will I be missing out on if I marry now?" "Do I need some time to discover more of life on my own?" "Will my friends think I'm insecure for marrying so young?"

"Maybe some will think I fear being alone?" Great questions! A quick Internet search can give you both the good and bad answers to all of those questions.

I hope to give you answers that are first and foremost biblical and Christ honoring. However, the answers you find in the Scriptures are the complete opposite of what you'll find through Google. With so many different answers out there, it's no surprise that people are uncertain and fearful of marriage.

Before we answer the obvious questions, let's get one thing out on the table: *Marrying young is not the problem.* Love is from our Lord. Being in love is a blessing. If God is arousing love in you for another and you plan to get married, we should be praising what He is doing, not telling you to wait unnecessarily.

Contrary to what you may have been told, marriage is not the reason people divorce. While I am an advocate for marrying young, I'm an even bigger advocate for helping you grow up. Experts call it "eradicating prolonged adolescence." And the *Young and in Love* message screams, "Take personal responsibility for your life!" Entering adulthood doesn't require that you wait until you're twenty-five years old, the age some researchers now believe is the milestone for adulthood. I don't want that for you because frankly it's unnecessary. Satan wants you to stay a little boy or girl because it leads you to focus on yourself and results in prolonged adolescence. But God wants you to press on to maturity.

I am blessed that I met my wife, Amy, at Liberty University, a school that was over-the-top pro-love and pro-dating. The founder of Liberty, Dr. Jerry Falwell, taught in chapel every Wednesday and regularly encouraged us not to kiss dating good-bye but to say hello and start asking girls out. Dr. Falwell went so far with this idea that he would often say, "If you're interested in a girl on this campus and she is dating someone else, but not yet engaged, then by all means ask her out." On one occasion he even said, "If the guy she is dating isn't committed enough to put a ring on her finger, he doesn't deserve her. Ask her out!" Thank You, Jesus, and thank you, Jerry. Jerry was not only an advocate for young marriage; he believed in a *competitive* dating scene.

So I did exactly as I was told!

Amy was twenty when we met, and I was twenty-one. She was in a serious relationship with a young ministry major. I knew it would be a challenge, but I tried to play it smooth. Now, this next part may cause you to stop reading and throw the book away, and I am okay with that. I didn't have the guts to ask her out myself, so I had my friend Austin Deloach set it up.

Austin was the senior-class president, and he didn't seem to enjoy the details that came with his office. I was the junior-class president, and I thrived on the organization and administration that came with mine. So in the spring of 1995, Austin asked me what he could do to help with the junior-senior cruise.

"Get me a date for the cruise with Amy Freitag," I said to him.

"Will do," he said. And that was that. He set me up on a blind date with Amy on Smith Mountain Lake outside of Lynchburg, Virginia.

That night I decided she was the one. Later, I told Austin that I would one day ask Amy to marry me, and I did. Twelve months later, in Fremont, Nebraska, after I asked for permission from Amy's dad, I presented Amy with a marquise-cut diamond ring. The karat size is an unnecessary detail, but keep in mind, I'd just graduated college. We were married on October 19, 1996. She was twenty-one, and I was twenty-two.

Never once did we think we were too young. Unprepared? *Yes.* Too young? No. Our parents blessed it. So did both of our churches. The idea that we needed to wait another five or even seven years, get good jobs, learn to be independent, and then settle down never once crossed our minds. For us, marriage was a milestone at the front end of adulthood, not the back end, and we genuinely looked forward to marriage and figuring out our lives together.

Shannon Fox, a marriage and family therapist and mom to my son's best friend, recently wrote a book called *Last One Down the Aisle Wins.* In her book, Shannon encourages young people to wait until at least age twenty-five before they marry. In her book, she writes:

> What if we told you that we know the key to more than doubling your chances of staying married? And what if we told you that this key was something you can use right now, whether you're single without a prospect in sight, in a serious relationship, or engaged to the love of your life and knee-deep in *Brides* magazines? How much would it be worth to you? Would it be worth five easy payments of $29.99 plus shipping and handling? Or how about just the price of this book?
>
> Here's the key: **Don't marry young.** In fact, don't get married until you're thirty. According

to the National Center for Health Statistics, your
chances of staying married more than double if you
get married after the age of twenty-five.[1]

Shannon is not alone in her advocacy for delayed marriage.
Campus pastors are challenging students to neglect young budding love in order to focus on their relationship with Christ.
Parents push the delay with bribes and the "you've got your whole
life ahead of you" argument. Friends encourage the delay for fear
of losing their buddies. Churches teach the delay as an antidote to
divorce. Young lovers delay marriage in order to give cohabitation
a shot. Young women delay in hopes of finding the perfect guy.
Young men delay to give themselves a few more years to party and
"sow their wild oats." Researchers give us their studies that show
the delay is best for your marital longevity and happiness.

I hate the delay, and I firmly believe it is unnecessary. My
heart is to validate young love and provide a framework to make
sure you are ready and the one you have chosen is *wedable*.
Ultimately, *Young and in Love* honors marriage and encourages
marriages in the making. This is not another purity book teaching
you how to suppress any and all feelings of love. No way! I want
you to express your love and then enjoy marriage.

So if you kissed dating good-bye, it's time to say hello! If you
have kept true love waiting, I tell you now, *wait no more*. Get
married!

The *Young and in Love* message comes with a warning label.
You are reading *Young and in Love*, not *Young and Looking for Love*
or *Young and Not Looking for Love*. Reader discretion is advised.

This book is not for the intentional single, the guy or gal who has decided not to marry. You will get extremely frustrated with this book.

This is not a dating book covering the how-tos of dating or courting.

This is not a book to give to your single friends and say, "Read this, find someone, and get married."

This is not a book about cohabitation.

This is not a book about the woes of society.

This book will not help you find a soul mate.

This book is not for the single person who wants to be married but can't find someone.

This is not an abstinence book with a purity message for your youth group.

This book is not intended to teach singles how to be content and productive while they wait patiently for God to send them the right person.

Then who is it for?

This book is for the single man or woman who is in love and wants to get married but is being told by everyone around him or her, "You're too young!" This book is for the person in his or her late teens or early twenties who needs to say "so long" to prolonged adolescence. If you are in love but the one you want to marry feels irresponsible marrying young, then I hope you both will be equipped to chase the foxes and avoid unnecessary delay.

This book is a primer for your premarital counseling. However, I won't make you sit in a pastor's office, burdening you with budgets, personality tests, or wedding planning. I want to challenge you to embrace maturity and adulthood at an early age. This book honors

Scripture. The Bible honors marriage, prepares us to be adults, and keeps family and friends from becoming foxes. I am a pastor. My heart is to bless your young love, correct, rebuke, and teach through Scripture. My daughter, Corynn, is seven years old, and my son, Carson, is five. She is my princess, and he is my mighty warrior. I advocate for young marriage with both of them in mind, and I do not take that lightly.

And finally, in all honesty, I hope this book starts a movement that honors marriage, eradicates prolonged adolescence, embraces adulthood, and builds lifelong committed marriages.

While there are many valid reasons to delay marriage, your age should not be on that list. Marriages fall apart for all sorts of reasons: unmet expectations, unrealistic expectations, buying into the "soul mate" myth, prolonged adolescence, lack of commitment, and a culture that devalues marriage. But to say those all go away with age is a fallacy. The issue is maturity, not age.

A Special Note to the Frustrated Female Reader

The purpose of this book is to help couples chase away the foxes of young love. Perhaps many single readers will set the book down in frustration. That is completely understandable. Several single women read this book toward the end of the writing process. Janae Bass, a young woman from our church, sent me the following message on Facebook:

> Okay, so I just finished reading your book *Young and in Love*. I really liked it a lot, and I agree that to be "young and in love" would be great. I know

that you said in the book and I've heard you say lots of times at church that men should be men and ask girls out. So my question is, what do you suggest for single girls in the meantime? I'm not a hermit; I'm involved at church and in the community. I don't sit in my apartment at night and wait for Prince Charming to knock on the door—but still no men.... If you have any advice for us single women while we wait for men to be men, please let me know.

When I read this message to my wife, she said, "Girls need to learn how to appropriately flirt." Her answer did not surprise me.

I get the frustration of waiting for men to initiate. I encouraged the young woman from our church to express her interest. And no, I do not consider showing interest and chasing the same thing. Flirting says, "I'm interested and would like to explore the possibilities." Chasing says, "I want you and will pursue you." Big difference! Showing and expressing interest in a guy can be extremely difficult for young women who have been raised to be independent and to allow men to take the lead. You may fear that flirting communicates desperation, weakness, or too much strength.

I believe God can use you in the maturing process of young men. He used Amy in my life to solidify my calling and vocation. It is absolutely permissible for you to begin spending time with a guy, whether you call that dating or something else, and expressing your interest. Don't allow your frustration over the immaturity of young men to turn your heart cold, aloof, or distant to the prospects of marriage.

Check out www.youngandinlove.com for video podcasts,
articles, and resources to help you prepare for marriage.

Young and in Love Marriage Journal

What are your beliefs about marriage and singleness?

*If you are young and in love, when did you know this
was the guy/gal you wanted to marry?*

What are several good reasons to delay marriage?

What are several bad reasons to delay marriage?

Fox Alerts

Throughout this book, "foxes" are not hot chicks. Foxes are individu-
als, groups, or things that seek to destroy or delay your blossoming
marriage. I have included twenty-four fox alerts in this book. As a
pastor, my role is that of shepherd and teacher, and in that role, I will
help you identify and protect yourself from these savage beasts. My
staff is in hand, and I am ready to go!

Chapter 2

Please, No More Purity Talks!

Marriage should be honored by all, and the marriage bed kept pure,
for God will judge the adulterer and all the sexually immoral.

—Hebrews 13:4

Marriage is the proper reward for a real lover, and
he is not a mercenary for desiring it.

—C. S. Lewis, *The Weight of Glory*

"Sex is dirty, nasty, and ugly, and you should save it for the one you love."

That was the purity talk I heard growing up in my independent, fundamental, premillenial, King-James-Version-Only Baptist church and home. That message was never spoken in those words, but it was all I heard.

I grew up in a home that loved Jesus and was committed to the Bible. My parents taught me the Scriptures, and we listened as my pastor preached them every Sunday morning, Sunday night, and Wednesday night. He preached that sex outside of marriage was sin. The words *sex, sin,* and *marriage* were often used in the same sentence. Sex quickly became a bad word. I grew up with great confusion about my body, sex, and the opposite sex. When I started noticing girls "in that way" I knew there was something wrong. Don't have sex. Don't masturbate. Pray.

Most of my friends in the church youth group succumbed to the evil and started sleeping around. Despite all of the purity rings, virginity pledges, and "Jesus, I'm sorry" prayers, they still had sex.

In many ways, we applied Hebrews 13:4 in reverse, reading it this way: "God will judge the adulterer and the sexually immoral, so don't have sex, and save it for marriage." Through all this, we heard even louder the messages, "Don't!" and "Wait!"

In truth, we were taught to honor celibacy and purity and *not* marriage.

I never heard the message, "God created us as sexual beings with gender-specific bodies and sexual desires." That part somehow got lost.

I will never forget the night my three-year-old son popped up out of the bathtub, looking at his penis, and asked me, "What is this?" Depending on the parent, there's more than one answer to that question.

"That is your tallywacker."

"That is your ying-a-ling."

Instead, with the authority of an apostle, I proclaimed, "That's your penis, Carson." I vaguely remember using a deep voice as well, and then I immediately walked out of the room.

Wouldn't you know it—that became Carson's new favorite word.

A few days later, Carson and I were eating at a local restaurant here in Branson, Missouri, a town of six thousand that entertains eight million tourists a year. Carson had flipped the place mat over and was drawing pictures. One sweet little old tourist lady came over to us and asked him, "Son, you are adorable—what are you drawing?"

My heart sank. Carson could see I was starting to make an excuse for what I thought was a very inappropriate drawing.

He looked up at me and said, "Dad, I'm drawing a dragon, not a penis."

It didn't look like a dragon.

Amy and I made the decision early not to teach our children that there is something weird about their bodies, desires, or sex. We refuse to use goofy expressions to describe body parts. We tell them the anatomically correct terms. As they grow up we will share with them what is appropriate and answer their questions appropriately.

For a lot of young people today, sex was not a subject discussed openly at home, let alone in the church. Parents and churches developed one simple purity message:

"Don't."

For the first three years of our marriage I struggled in the sex department. I undressed under the covers in a dark bedroom because I carried a deep-seated belief that sex was wrong. I was a virgin when I got married but still had those moments when I asked the question, "Is this okay?"

I was led to believe that a wedding ceremony would flip a switch in my thinking about sex as something dirty or shame-based, changing it to something wonderful and erotic. Boy, was I wrong.

God's plan from the beginning has always been to delay sex until marriage. But we've turned it around. Now, singles are delaying marriage and having sex. One hundred years ago, pastors believed sex before marriage was morally wrong. Today, every evangelical pastor I know still believes it, and this teaching hasn't changed in our churches. But do you know what has changed? Our ideas about marriage. And they've changed a lot. Mark Regnerus wrote in *Christianity Today*,

> Parents and pastors and youth group leaders told us not to do it before we got married … [b]ecause the Bible says so. Yet that simple message didn't go very far…. The message must change….[1]

For the majority of young people, purity talks are not working. To fix them should we change what we believe about purity? Absolutely not! In our churches and homes we need to repackage the message and refocus on *honoring marriage*. We have minimized the beauty of desire, our bodies, and covenantal heterosexual marriage. And in the meantime, Satan has stepped through the crack in the door and duped us into believing that *marriage* is the problem. Men and women cannot make it together, so they should avoid the institution altogether.

Our message must change. The church must sound the trumpet of marriage and let every young person know that the desire to be with someone of the opposite sex is good and healthy and God-given. We practice self-discipline to enjoy and honor one of God's greatest gifts: *holy marriage*.

Duped by a Demonic Doctrine

Sexual desire comes from our Lord. We were created as sexual beings. Marriage is God's plan for enjoying sexual intimacy. Marriage and sex are gifts to us from God.

In 1 Timothy 4, the apostle Paul confronted a teaching of the Gnostics. In that day the Gnostics taught that the material world was evil. They taught that to keep our lives pure, we must avoid certain practices, and unfortunately, they took that which God created and perverted it. Paul, an older preacher, instructed Timothy, a younger pastor, to hit them right between the eyes for their lies:

> The Spirit clearly says that in later times some will abandon the faith and follow deceiving spirits and things taught by demons. Such teachings come through hypocritical liars, whose consciences have been seared as with a hot iron. They forbid people to marry and order them to abstain from certain foods, which God created to be received with thanksgiving by those who believe and who know the truth. For everything God created is good, and nothing is to be rejected if it is received with thanksgiving, because it is consecrated by the word of God and prayer. (vv. 1–5)

The first demonic teaching is in Genesis 3 when Satan spoke, through a serpent, to Eve. God forbid them to eat the fruit of the tree. Satan told Eve, "You will not surely die…. For God knows that when you eat of it your eyes will be opened, and you will be like God" (vv. 4–5).

Since that deception, every demonic lie goes back to the root of being your own god: "You can call your own shots, you can do your own thing, and you can justify your own soul. There's no such thing as a God you worship; *you can be God.*" Even saying, "Take charge of your life; do your own thing," is a demonic doctrine, so to speak.

Such teaching comes from hypocritical liars. The word *hypocrite* comes from a Greek term popularly used of actors in plays in ancient Greece. The actors portrayed certain parts on stage, but when they left the stage, they were entirely different people. That idea translates into the church today: Some keep up the appearance of being Christians, showing up for one hour a week on Sunday morning, but when they leave the church building, they act like who they really are. In 1 Timothy 4, Paul said that they are hypocritical liars whose conscience has been seared as with a hot iron.

The hypocritical priests that Paul referred to here taught that the single life was more favorable to God and that it would lead to perfection. That was also the favorite sentiment of some Jewish sects of the time. They preached singleness and told people, "Don't get married." Later it became the predominant practice in the Roman Catholic Church, which required its clergy to remain single and celibate and to take a vow to do so.

The Gnostics actually taught that marriage, certain foods, and possessions were evil and should be avoided. Paul called this unnecessary abstention a doctrine of demons. What God created is good and is to be enjoyed by all believers. We are to honor marriage because it was consecrated, sanctified, and set apart from the beginning of creation. We receive marriage as a gift from God because we know it's a spiritual issue. Paul implored Timothy not to allow the church to abandon these central teachings, which included honoring marriage as normative in the life of a believer.

Now, I hope you don't hear me calling advocates of delayed marriage evil. Some are simply misled. But still some others are false teachers. I believe they need to be warned about teaching abstinence from marriage in the same way Timothy warned the Gnostics. And I would go so far as to say that encouraging young people to abstain from marriage falls into the category of a demonic doctrine. Don't let politically correct terms fool you. Terms like feminism, cohabitation, independence, and liberation can trip you up. Take them for what they truly are: false teachings that dishonor marriage.

The apostle Paul referred to the union between a man and woman in marriage as a "profound mystery" (Eph. 5:32), which serves as a model of Christ and His bride, the church. The way a man and woman come together in marriage models the gospel of Jesus.

In the beginning, God created humankind in His image and likeness: "Let us make man in our image, in our likeness" (Gen. 1:26). This doesn't necessarily refer to the physical likeness of God as much as it does the emotional, intellectual, and relational attributes of God.

Genesis 2:18 begins, "The LORD God said, 'It is not good for the man to be alone.'" This is the only time in the creative order that God declared something as "not good." God created marriage as the normative state for humankind. In other words, we are better off when we have someone with us. Then God said, "I will make a helper suitable for him." The word *helper* implies that the man needs someone to come alongside him where he is lacking. The Hebrew word for *helper* in Genesis 2:18 is *ezer*, which means "one who helps." In fact, it's the same word used in Psalms 33:20; 70:1; and 115:9 when the writer refers to God. God gave Eve to Adam to come alongside him to assist; she does not come in front or behind him, but alongside.

After God decided that it was not good for man to be alone, He caused the man to fall into a deep sleep (Gen. 2:21). While he was sleeping, God took out one of the man's ribs and closed up the place with flesh. Then God made a woman from the rib He took from the man (v. 22). Genesis 2:23 says, "The man said, 'This is now bone of my bones and flesh of my flesh; she shall be called "woman," for she was taken out of man.'" Adam now had a spiritual, emotional, physical, and sexual companion.

This was the first and most prominent marriage in the Bible. But God gives us another example of marriage in Scripture in the Song of Songs. It offers more detail on the early stages of love and a marriage in the making.

The Shullamite Woman and Solomon

Sexual desire and attraction is part of God's design in you. We see in Song of Songs that the Shullamite woman felt a strong desire for Solomon. She wanted him to act on this desire quickly. There was no delay found in her love and desire for her newfound shepherd king:

> Let him kiss me with the kisses of his mouth—
> for your love is more delightful than wine.

> Pleasing is the fragrance of your perfumes;
>> your name is like perfume poured out.
> No wonder the maidens love you!
> Take me away with you—let us hurry!
> Let the king bring me into his chambers. (Song
> 1:2–4)

Not only did she want to go into the bedroom, but she said, "Let us hurry!" The Hebrew term there for "hurry" is "bom-bom-chicky-chicky-bom-bom."

I would be lying if I told you that I did not want to hurry off with Amy and "be" with her on the night we met. She is hot! She's even admitted to me that she thought I was pretty cute, but I can't get her to confess the hurry part.

Sexual attraction and desire for one's spouse honors marriage, and don't let anyone tell you any differently. It validates what God created in you. We must not suppress the desire but rather learn self-discipline within it.

If sexual attraction honors marriage, then observers of budding love should honor and praise what God is doing. Parents, pastors, campus leaders, friends, and family should "rejoice and delight in you; we will praise your love more than wine" (Song 1:4). Maybe your parents and married friends have forgotten how their own young love once felt.

It's obvious when sexual attraction is there, which I call "sparks." Like the bits of hot metal flying off the end of a welder's torch, your attraction and desire send out the sparks. You can see the sparks if you are ever in an airport when an eHarmony.

com couple meets for the first time. It's so obvious. Perhaps he's standing just outside of security with flowers or a small gift as she comes out of baggage claim. On more than one occasion I've turned to Amy at an airport and said, "Check it out, an eHarmony couple."

"How do you know?" she asks.

"Look at how the guy is stretching his neck wanting to get the first peek of the one he has known for months but has never met. Do you see any of those other men doing that?" I say.

Then the whole scene unfolds in front of us like a slow-motion clip from a movie. They embrace, and the sparks fly. I love it! I actually feel like I should hand them eight or nine bucks for the scene. I'm a sucker for that kind of romance.

Even when the sparks are flying, we tend to act in a way that guards our hearts from being rejected. When two people start dating, they don't typically share all the junk on the first date. They may wait a little while before sharing all of their secrets and shadows. The focus early in the relationship is on similarities, as couples downplay differences, struggles, and the past.

As in most first attractions, we ask the question, "Will this person accept me?" Being uncertain of that answer can create insecurity, and insecurity is part of almost all new relationships. Not only do we wonder if he or she will accept us, but we also have to wonder if others, such as parents and friends, will accept our relationship.

Like you and me early in a relationship, the Shullamite woman had insecurities. Perhaps you can relate to the struggles she had with her body and her family:

> Dark am I, yet lovely,
>> O daughters of Jerusalem,
>> dark like the tents of Kedar,
>> like the tent curtains of Solomon.
> Do not stare at me because I am dark,
>> because I am darkened by the sun.
> My mother's sons were angry with me
>> and made me take care of the vineyards;
>> my own vineyard I have neglected. (Song 1:5–6)

In Solomon's day, suntans were not in style. Paleness was considered beautiful. Why was she dark? As we see here, her brothers had an attitude and forced her to work outside. You can see her disdain for her brothers because she called them her "mother's sons." Her coerced labor caused her to work out in the sun, which tanned her skin. She had a desire for Solomon but believed he would not be interested in her because of her looks.

I have counseled many young women who have rushed into marriage to escape a bad family life. This is not a healthy reason to marry young. Leaving home is an essential ingredient for healthy marriage, but it should not be the stand-alone reason.

Some young women I've counseled have given themselves sexually to a guy to try to secure the commitment to the relationship. I've picked up the broken pieces in many young marriages because of this very issue. She felt she was going to lose him or that other girls were prettier, peppier, or more the marrying type. Ladies, sex is a horrible way to keep a guy or deal with your insecurities.

Even though the Shullamite woman dealt with strong insecurities, she chose to keep her character intact:

> Tell me, you whom I love, where you graze your flock
>   and where you rest your sheep at midday.
> Why should I be like a veiled woman
>   beside the flocks of your friends? (Song 1:7)

She told him that she would not be like a prostitute and meet up with him during his break from tending the sheep. Some women may use sex to medicate their struggles or please their men, but not her. She wouldn't bend her character.

Real men do not take advantage of women. Solomon could have taken advantage of her insecurities, but he did not. He didn't add to her struggles and pain by using her or taking advantage of her. Instead, he affirmed her and built security into their soon-to-be marriage:

> I liken you, my darling, to a mare
>   harnessed to one of the chariots of Pharaoh.
> Your cheeks are beautiful with earrings,
>   your neck with strings of jewels.
> We will make you earrings of gold,
>   studded with silver. (Song 1:9–11)

To compare your girlfriend or fiancée to a horse would probably not be a good idea, unless you lived in Solomon's day. When Solomon likened her to the mare among Pharaoh's chariots (v. 9), he used an emotional word picture to communicate the fact that she was beautiful. When Pharaoh and his army showed up to battle, dark horses pulled all of the chariots except for the Pharaoh's; instead, gorgeous white horses pulled his chariot and set him apart from all on the battlefield. Solomon turned the dark imagery she started with around on her. She stood out among all the women, even the veiled women outside the tents of his friends at midday.

When you're young and in love, not only do you have strong sexual attraction, but then a kind of fixation sets in. Scripture refers to this strong passion as a form of intoxication. When Amy and I were dating, she was all I could think about. Studying became almost impossible because I couldn't get her out of my mind. I thought of her first thing in the morning and would fall asleep at night talking to her on the phone. The Shullamite woman felt the exact same thing:

> While the king was at his table,
>> my perfume spread its fragrance.
> My lover is to me a sachet of myrrh
>> resting between my breasts.
> My lover is to me a cluster of henna blossoms
>> from the vineyards of En Gedi (Song 1:12–14).

We have the blessing of bathing every day in our society. After a long day we can step into a bath or shower with a plethora of soaps and shampoos right there on the ledge. Bathing wasn't that convenient three thousand years ago. Bathing was infrequent. Instead, they used perfumes, flowers, spices, and ancient versions of potpourri to keep themselves smelling good. And these scents would linger. The

Shullamite woman compared Solomon to a pouch of blossoms and perfumes that she tied around her neck. In that day, women would wear spices and blossoms to bed at night to permeate their bodies while they slept. In essence, she fell asleep at night and awakened in the morning with thoughts of him lingering.

Marriage author Gary Chapman calls this "in love" experience "the tingles." The tingles are perfectly normal and part of young love. If you start feeling the tingles toward someone while you're in school, there's a good chance your grades will be affected. It's hard to keep your mind on the history of World War II, the Bill of Rights, or the Declaration of Independence when your thoughts are consumed with the next date.

When love is growing, sex is delayed but desire is not. A new couple begins to have deep, intimate conversations about the marriage and life they will experience together in the not-so-distant future. This kind of conversation builds security. In the Song of Songs, the dialogue turned to imagery about the home they would share one day:

Solomon:
How beautiful you are, my darling!
Oh, how beautiful!
Your eyes are doves.

Shullamite:
How handsome you are, my lover!
Oh, how charming!
And our bed is verdant.

Solomon:
> The beams of our house are cedars;
> our rafters are firs. (Song 1:15–17)

He wasn't describing the type of wood he would use to build their home. He was making the statement that their home would be a mansion of security. It would be a safe place. He could be trusted.

Their young love progressed quickly. She started their relationship with insecurity, he built her up, and she was then able to say:

> I am a rose of Sharon,
> a lily of the valleys. (Song 2:1)

That's a far cry from, "Do not stare at me because I am dark, because I am darkened by the sun." She grew personally, and their relationship was part of that process. Some would have you believe that you need to deal with your insecurities prior to any serious relationship or marriage. Solomon and the Shullamite woman are a perfect example of how a relationship can help you grow your character and deal with your "stuff." Can independence and singleness do that? Sure. But so can the deep commitment and maturity of a growing young love. Solomon built her up even further by using the metaphor of a flower among thorns:

> Like a lily among thorns
> is my darling among the maidens. (Song 2:2)

Reassuring her of his love, he recognized her growth despite a challenging past. Not all of the women around her were successful, but she flourished among them.

No doubt you have witnessed failing marriages and the failed relationships of your friends. The reasons for failure are numerous. You have seen many thorns, but you can grow despite the statistics and examples. You can be a lily among thorns.

Just as Solomon praised his bride-to-be, she in turn called out his character:

> Like an apple tree among the trees of the forest
>   is my lover among the young men.
> I delight to sit in his shade,
>   and his fruit is sweet to my taste.
> He has taken me to the banquet hall,
>   and his banner over me is love. (Song 2:3–4)

She received nourishment from him. There were a lot of men for her to choose from, which she referred to as the other trees of the forest.

This summer in Branson has set records for hot days. We have had consecutive days of 100-plus-degree heat with heat indexes reaching as high as 108 degrees. On those days, you seek out shade. The shade of a tree can provide temperatures 20 degrees cooler than the sunny spots. Have you ever experienced the "ahhhh" moment of stepping into the shade on a hot summer day? What could be better? How about a light snack? Now we've hit man's two primary buttons: *rest and food.*

Many men were available for shade, but Solomon came with a treat—like reaching up and picking an apple to eat while resting. I love it! She called Solomon a little snack. Maybe that's why pet names so often refer to food (e.g., cupcake, sweetie, sugar). Bom-bom-chicky-chicky-bom-bom.

However, the Shullamite woman did not desire a little snack. Her attraction and desire were so strong that she wanted a feast:

> Strengthen me with raisins,
>> refresh me with apples,
>> for I am faint with love.
> His left arm is under my head,
>> and his right arm embraces me.
> Daughters of Jerusalem, I charge you
>> by the gazelles and by the does of the field:
> Do not arouse or awaken love
>> until it so desires. (Song 2:5–7)

Although she wanted the aphrodisiacs of raisins and to be filled with his love, it was not yet the proper time to awaken love. This is the strongest mention of delay in the text so far. They would not awaken love until family and friends recognized their commitment to one another. We call that a wedding.

Their ceremony was right around the corner. The Shullamite woman anticipated this union and pictured their maturing love. Winter was passing, and spring brought with it the blossoms:

> Listen! My lover!
> Look! Here he comes,

leaping across the mountains,
>   bounding over the hills.
My lover is like a gazelle or a young stag.
>   Look! There he stands behind our wall,
gazing through the windows,
>   peering through the lattice.
My lover spoke and said to me,
>   "Arise, my darling,
>   my beautiful one, and come with me.
See! The winter is past;
>   the rains are over and gone.
Flowers appear on the earth;
>   the season of singing has come,
the cooing of doves
>   is heard in our land.
The fig tree forms its early fruit;
>   the blossoming vines spread their fragrance.
Arise, come, my darling;
>   my beautiful one, come with me. (Song 2:8–13)

Dating is all about *curiosity* and *fascination*. We spend countless hours getting to know the one we love. We ask great questions and dive deep into his or her heart. The shepherd king painted a wonderful word picture of this stage of love:

My dove in the clefts of the rock,
>   in the hiding places on the mountainside,
show me your face,

let me hear your voice;
   for your voice is sweet,
      and your face is lovely. (Song 2:14)

Solomon was saying, "I want to get to know you." He loved it when she spoke and told him about herself. He wanted to communicate with her.

One of the greatest strengths of young lovers is that this curiosity comes naturally. We're intrigued by one another and desire to connect on deeper levels. Marriage brings with it the new components of *duty* and *responsibility*. When you are dating, you don't share bills, household chores, or child-rearing responsibilities. The key, once you are married, is not to *replace* curiosity and fascination with duty and responsibility. We must balance them all.

Up to this point, everything was going well with Solomon and the Shullamite woman. But there were outside influences that could destroy the beauty of what spring was producing:

Catch for us the foxes,
   the little foxes
that ruin the vineyards,
      our vineyards that are in bloom. (Song 2:15)

The foxes of young budding love are too numerous to list. Myths, false doctrines, pride, selfishness, prolonged adolescence, parents, youth pastors, teachers, the church, and even you yourself can ruin the young buds of love. The Shullamite woman and Solomon were responsible for guarding their love and marriage from these foxes.

My primary concern is that you do not become a fox to your own vineyard. Your young marriage will have plenty of foxes to contend with, but you don't need to be one of them.

Next, the Shullamite woman invited her young lover to enjoy her body. He would, but only after the wedding, which is described in Song of Songs 3:

> My lover is mine and I am his;
> > he browses among the lilies.
> Until the day breaks
> > and the shadows flee,
> turn, my lover,
> > and be like a gazelle
> or like a young stag
> > on the rugged hills. (Song 2:16–17)

There is nothing better than to be young and in love. I regularly encourage the men of our congregation to watch young couples in public. Watch the way they hold hands, gently touch, and show chivalry. It is inspiring, and some of us old guys have forgotten what that felt like. And when the young lovers begin to nauseate us, we find ourselves as old, grumpy foxes dishonoring marriage.

Foxes and Beetles

We do not have a fox problem where we live in southwest Missouri. I can grow a garden with no threat of foxes eating my tomatoes. But every day in June and July I ask my Father in heaven, "Why did You create the Japanese beetle?"

I can't figure it out. They descend on my garden, ornamental plants, and my favorite purple plum tree every summer. I hang beetle bags around the perimeter of my yard. These bags are meant to last all summer long, but each bag fills up in less than forty-eight hours. I personally executed some forty to fifty thousand Japanese beetles last summer alone. I spray an insecticide, but with rain and sprinklers, my garden requires almost daily treatment.

We've lived in this house for three years, and I have yet to see my favorite plant fully bloom. It's an Althea shrub. Have you ever seen one of those? The buds are huge, and the blooms are a vibrant red. Early in the summer, I had several hundred buds on that shrub, some of which were the size of golf balls. I declared before the Lord this year that it would actually bloom, that the beetles wouldn't touch it.

I kept the little suckers off the buds through most of June, but once they devoured the purple plum tree the beetles moved over and started munching on my prize Althea. A dozen or so buds eventually bloomed, but hundreds were lost to the beetles.

If we're not careful as parents, friends, and church members, we can become like that Japanese beetle. We might see a young couple falling in love, and we start munching. We never see the bloom because we are so preoccupied with destroying the bud. *Do not arouse or awaken love until it so desires* (Song 2:7) means we leave the bud so that it may eventually bloom on its own.

Professor Mark Regnerus said this: "We would do well to recognize *some* of these relationships [as] marriages in the making."[2]

We must let buds of love form. If we feed them well and protect them, spring will usher in the bloom we call marriage. That is how we esteem marriage as highly valuable. That is how the church is to honor holy matrimony.

Check out www.youngandinlove.com for video podcasts, articles, and resources to help you prepare for marriage.

Young and in Love Marriage Journal

What have you been taught about sex and marriage?

Describe the attraction you are currently feeling.

How is this attraction different from attractions from your past?

How is it the same?

Can you identify any early foxes? Who or what are they? (Keep in mind, this list may change as you move through the book.)

Fox Alert: The Church

Most pastors I know are at a loss about what to do to keep couples together in their congregations. We get louder, preach harder, and offer the couple a longer period of dating and engagement to make sure they are ready.

We must remember that we can destroy young buds by:

- Creating man-made restrictions or qualifications to marriage
- Honoring a college education above marriage
- Agreeing with parents who are longtime givers to the church
- Setting arbitrary age limits on maturity

Chapter 3

The Tone

He who finds a wife finds what is good and receives favor from the Lord.
—Proverbs 18:22

Justin's text message was my first-ever digital engagement announcement. In sixty-eight characters he wrote, "Just got engaged. She said yes. Can u believe it? Can't wait! Will u do the wedding?"

I responded with, "You'll love being married! It's gr8! You r a fantastic couple. Proud of u J and J!"

Justin and Jocelyn could be models for that little couple that sits atop the wedding cake. He's twenty-three. She's twenty-one. Justin is a professional magician, top hat and all, who has graced stages in Branson and Las Vegas and on countless cruise liners. Jocelyn is finishing up her schooling to become a counselor.

Since I'm more Justin's friend than his pastor, he started mentioning the big *M* word to me several months before he asked Jocelyn. I asked all the appropriate questions like, "Is she a follower of Jesus?" "Does she have a temper?" and "Have you known her long enough to see what really sets her off?" You know, the basic "should I walk down the aisle?" type stuff. His answers were spot-on. No red flags. No yellow lights.

A few weeks after their engagement, Amy and I had Justin and Jocelyn over for dinner and their first premarital session. Counseling engaged couples is a riot for me. I have a technique for young couples that probably wouldn't be approved by the American Association of Christian Counselors. After years of counseling engaged couples, I was exhausted by the fact that they never fight, have everything in common, and think their differences are cute. So now I "fix" the sessions much like a boxer throwing a fight for his bookies.

The plan is simple. Amy and I host the couple for the first session but give them bad directions to our house. Couples usually call us thirty minutes late in a panicked voice. My goal is to completely frustrate them so hopefully they will show up mad. It's even better if they walk in the door blaming each other for taking down bad directions or not following them correctly. Now we can get somewhere.

My plan didn't work on Justin. I quickly learned that I would not be teaching Justin a whole lot that night. His excitement for marriage oozed out of every pore of his body. He had already attended two marriage conferences and read half a dozen books prior to popping the question. I don't know whether to call him a teacher's pet, poster child, hopeless romantic, or marriage dweeb. Nevertheless, he was anxious and excited for marriage.

Most couples anticipate the wedding. It's rare these days to meet a young couple excited about paying bills, taking on a mortgage, and balancing life and work, but Justin and Jocelyn were that couple.

After dinner, Justin performed a few table magic tricks for our kids, and then we dived right in. Justin told us, "Ted, you were the only one excited for us when we announced our engagement."

"What?" I said with shock.

"Yeah, our parents encouraged us to not rush things and said maybe we should give it a little more time. Our friends couldn't understand why we would want to give up our freedom in singleness. You were the only one who jumped up and down for us."

Justin's friends and family have *the tone*, and they're not an anomaly. I am beginning to feel the same sentiment around the country. My alma mater, Liberty University, invites me back each year to speak at convocation. My subject is always tied to marriage. I remember being a student at Liberty and hearing countless talks each year on purity. To be frank, I grew exhausted by these talks. Don't hear me say that I am down on purity. I'm not. I'm down on the relentless pursuit to make chastity hip while ignoring marriage when talking to students.

My returns to conservative, evangelical Liberty University have opened my ears to a tone among twentysomethings. The tone goes something like this: "I need to protect my future from marriage." I hear the tone come out in statements like:

> "We have so many divorces in our society today because couples are marrying too early."

"I want to settle into my career before settling down in marriage."

"My girlfriend and I have different career pursuits, and we're afraid that marriage right now could sabotage both our futures."

"I know the right guy will come along, but I'm not looking or pursuing any serious relationships."

"I'm not ready for marriage."

"I was ready to marry him, but he wasn't ready."

"He needs to figure out what he's going to do in life before we take our relationship to the next level."

Did you pick up on *the tone?* It's not a mean or frustrated tone; it's just a tone.

On average, we are marrying later, if at all. We have adapted to getting our life in order first and marrying last. We don't want a spouse to screw up our plans or to tweak them. We're independent thinkers, and establishing our career is important for our future success. We also protect our future from the patterns our parents have set, from prolonged adolescence, and from cultural pressures. All three are pulling you away from marriage itself, let alone early marriage.

Your Parents' Marriage

The tone starts early in life. It starts at home. Your parents impressed a particular set of marriage beliefs—good, bad, or indifferent—deep into your heart. You had a front-row seat to their marriage. You watched a side of their relationship that their bosses, friends at church, and neighbors never saw. Maybe the better word picture is that you got to see what went on in the locker room, not just what happened on the field.

As a pastor, I have responded with alarm to the statistics showing young people leaving the church at age eighteen. I've heard countless reasons for this exodus, but frankly the main reason has been diminished in the dialogue. Churches are spending more on youth programs, hiring more staff, and teaching deeper commitment, but the eighteen-year-olds are still leaving. Why? Are they leaving the hypocrisy of the church? Or are they leaving the hypocrisy of the home? I think the answer is the latter, not the former.

I do not believe young people are rebelling against the church as much as they are searching for an authentic, genuine model from the people who took them to church in the first place. They often look at their parents' marriage and say, "I don't want that. There must be a better way."

You may be thinking, *Yeah, but my parents didn't start off that way. Were they compatible and deep in love early on, and then later drifted apart?*

Maybe, but marriage is not to blame. They are. They allowed things to drift and grew apart. Some couples of the Boomer generation seem to value commitment over fun. Yes, I said it—fun! God calls us to commitment, true, but did He call us to a committed, stinky marriage? No. But how many couples today believe they have a good Christian marriage so long as they stay together?

If your parents haven't modeled a healthy relationship, know that your parents' marriage does not have to be yours. You choose whether or not you drift apart from your spouse. You may need to get rid of your parents' definition of marriage and embrace one that is more biblical: *a lifetime commitment between a husband and wife who enjoy life and each other.*

Prolonged Adolescence

Scripturally and historically, there are two life phases in the development of a young man: *child* and then *man*. This transition was explained by the apostle Paul when he wrote, "When I was a child, I talked like a child, I thought like a child, I reasoned like a child. When I became a man, I put childish ways behind me" (1 Cor. 13:11).

Going from a child to a man meant:

- Leaving home (Gen. 2:24)
- Graduating from school
- Getting a job
- Marrying a woman
- Starting a family

All five of these milestones happened quickly, if not simultaneously. Nowhere in Scripture can you find a wide gap between childhood and adulthood. But today, we have created one. It is called adolescence.

Adolescence starts in the early teen years and for some continues on into the thirties. Young people today are confused about when and how to grow up, and their parents, churches, and culture place zero pressure on them to do so.

Prolonged adolescence for many is an extended vacation from responsibility. Marriage is a huge responsibility, and many young people delay it in order to party more, drink more, enjoy more lovers, make money, get established in a good job, and enjoy their freedom. The tone of our culture says, "Why would I want to get married and mess with the good thing I've got going?" That's an honest question because marriage and adolescence don't mix well.

I love everything about weddings. From the processional to the ceremony to the reception, who doesn't love an all-day party? The only thing I don't like about weddings is the prep and rehearsal. The groomsmen often show up late. Family must be introduced to one another. Things move slowly. And everyone has an opinion about how the wedding party should stand or how they should come down the aisle. I operate on two fundamental beliefs: First, the bride's opinion is the only one that matters, and second, I am in charge. If you believe in those two, then we'll have a great rehearsal.

Several summers ago I was asked to perform the wedding of Jessica Paul. She is the daughter of my good friend Dr. Bob Paul, president of the National Institute of Marriage. Bob was nervous but ready to marry off his eldest daughter. They made a great father-daughter pair. Bob is tall and sharp, and Jessica is a professional model. The rehearsal started on time, and we were flowing until Bob gave me his opinion.

"Bob! What are you doing?" I said with sarcastic exhaustion. We're friends, so I can get away with a lot.

"I have some theology behind the unity candle that I want to make sure is worked into the message," he insisted. We were in trouble. I've had brides' moms share with me how I should stand, photographers tell me to move, and dads ask me to keep it short. But never have I been told what to say. I looked at Bob in shock.

Bob took the next few minutes during the rehearsal to share his view: "The way we teach the unity candle communicates a false truth about marriage. Typically, the bride and groom light the middle candle representing their oneness, then blow out the individual candles. All I am asking is that they do not blow out their individual candles."

"Bob, do we need to get into this right now?" I asked.

His passion for the candle remained. "Ted, do you know what we are saying when we blow out the individual candles? We are saying that oneness trumps and removes their individual responsibility to grow in the Lord. The candles on that table need to represent three spiritual journeys: Jessica's journey, Chris's journey, and their marital journey."

While I wanted to argue with him and call him Martin Luther for being such a reformer, I actually heeded his words. They made good, biblical sense to me.

Your mom and dad are responsible for their individual spiritual journeys. You are responsible for your own individual journey. What you may have witnessed growing up was a lax approach to spiritual growth. Maybe your parents allowed work, duty, responsibility, you, and your siblings to keep them from enjoying life with each other. If so, they forgot to prioritize their marriage above all and settled into a self-centered lifestyle that is the opposite of our biblical call to submit to one another out of reverence for Christ (Eph. 5).

Marriage is part of growing up. And in that process, guard your heart from this self-centered tone. Singles often use words like *calling* and *gift* to describe their decision not to marry. You will know whether your singleness will serve Christ or whether it is meant to serve you. Therefore, don't use singleness as an excuse to prolong your own adolescence; rather, honor Christ with your life and honor marriage.

Our Culture

There's a real tension between marriage and maturity, and for our culture, one of the most popular sitcoms of all time clearly defined this tension. I cringed when I heard *the tone* on an episode of *Seinfeld,* in which Jerry decides he's a child and needs to grow up. About time, Jerry! So he seeks out advice on maturity from the great theologian Kramer.

"I had a very interesting lunch with George…. We both kind of realized we're kids. We're not men," Jerry begins.

Kramer replies, "So then you asked yourselves, 'Is there something more to life?'"

"Yes! We did!" Jerry says.

"Yeah, well, let me clue you in on something: There isn't…. What are you thinking about, Jerry? Marriage? Family?" Kramer asks.

Jerry responds, "Well …"

Kramer says with his signature strut, "They're prisons! Manmade prisons. You're doing time! You get up in the morning, she's there. You go to sleep at night, she's there. It's like you gotta ask permission to use the bathroom."

Jerry replies, "I'm glad we had this talk."

Kramer responds, "Oh, you have no idea."[1]

Kramer is speaking for an entire generation of people who are delaying marriage. But I say, why wait? Why the delay? Do you really have to choose between life and a wife? Prolonged adolescence does not mean that we must delay marriage. Marriage is the greatest tool on earth for maturing us and making each of us more like Jesus. Trade in clichéd thinking like "the old ball and chain," "whipped," and "doing time." Instead, trade those ideas for a marriage that will help you enjoy life and your spouse.

Unchecked, *the tone* will make you smug. I drive the singles in my church crazy with my constant "start dating and get married" soapbox. Little boys in their twenties drive me insane because they sit in our congregation week after week surrounded by well-qualified young women, and yet they refrain from asking them out. I'm in my thirties, but these guys look at me like I am an old man giving them a "back in the day" speech.

The Bible has a tone about marriage and family, and I can assure you, it's very different from what you've heard from Mom, Dad, friends, our culture, and even some churches. I thought I was going to split our church on the Sunday I challenged the single guys to start asking out our single moms. I spoke with a tone that many commented on as, "Something they have never heard come out of a pastor's mouth."

Hot Mamas

I'm constantly looking for new ways to shock the congregation at Woodland Hills. It doesn't take much, and I don't have to be all that creative; the Bible offers me plenty of opportunities. One particular text caused quite a stir at our church and freaked out many of our singles. I was reminded how easily we embrace the world's values for marriage and outright reject God's.

During the summer of 2010 I preached through the New Testament book of 1 Timothy. It is a letter written from an old pastor to a young pastor who is struggling to keep a church healthy. Paul encouraged young Timothy with a how-to manual on worship, leadership, and caring for the overall church family. One of the practical teachings of that book is a radical approach to caring for single moms in the church. Paul's solution? Get married. This is probably not a solution your parents or our culture has ever taught you.

This passage teaches that single moms over the age of sixty with no family to care for them should become a ministry of the church:

> No widow may be put on the list of widows unless she is over sixty, has been faithful to her husband, and is well known for her good deeds, such as bringing up children, showing hospitality, washing the feet of the saints, helping those in trouble and devoting herself to all kinds of good deeds. (1 Tim. 5:9–10)

We have a lot of single moms at Woodland Hills Family Church who have been deserted by their husbands. These men had an affair and left for the other woman or just decided to leave without cause. They left their wives and children high and dry. These men are bums. Frankly, I'm furious at the church for picking up the pieces for little boys who can't man up and care for their own families. These guys even have the nerve to fight the courts over how much their kids should get in child-support payments. When I meet a guy who is fighting the courts on how much he should pay to take care of his kids, I want to, in pastoral love, break his nose. I can't believe he's really fighting over how much money his kids should get. He should go without, live in a one-room apartment or on the couch of a friend. He's deserted his wife and now wants to force her to scrape by for the rest of her life?

Young men are deserting young women. At Woodland Hills we have single moms as young as twenty-one years old. What do we say to the twenty-one-year-old single mom? *Get married.* Single moms and fatherless children need husbands and fathers. Here's where the feminists will go all nutty wacky on me. But twenty-one-year-old single moms do not need to be placed on a list for the church to show benevolence. Instead, the young men of the church need to marry them. Paul went on:

> As for younger widows, do not put them on such a list. For when their sensual desires overcome their dedication to Christ, they want to marry. Thus they bring judgment on themselves, because they have broken their first pledge. Besides, they get into the habit of being idle and going about from house to house. And not only do they become idlers, but also gossips and busybodies, saying things they ought not to. So I counsel younger widows to marry, to have children, to manage their homes and to give the

enemy no opportunity for slander. Some have in fact
already turned away to follow Satan. (1 Tim. 5:11–15)

Do you know what single moms at Woodland Hills Family
Church need? They need husbands. Do you know what the fatherless
children at Woodland Hills need? They don't need another government program; *they need dads.*

May we never (I'm going where angels dare not tread) look at
single motherhood as ideal or normative as a church. A movie called
The Switch, starring Jennifer Aniston, does just that. It's a comedy,
but the thread that runs through the movie is "Women do not need
men to have babies." Speaking of the plot, Aniston said, "Women
are realizing more and more that you don't have to settle. They don't
have to fiddle with a man to have that child…. They are realizing
that if it's that time in their life and they want this part they can do
it with or without that."[2]

The Hebrew term for that is *baloney*. It's absolute silliness. It's
a demonic doctrine, and Satan has packaged it in this thing called
feminism. God's plan is for single moms to get married.

I constantly challenge the young men of our church to consider
single moms when choosing a mate. Some of you are thinking, *What
kind of freaky cult is Ted leading out there in Branson?* Give me just a
second, and don't check out on me just yet. Some young men over-
look great women in the church because of their so-called baggage.
They don't want to deal with stepchildren or ex-husbands. But I must
say, single moms are not damaged goods. Again, in the Hebrew the
word is *baloney.* It takes a real man to marry a woman with children.
It takes a man who embraces responsibility *and* maturity.

Some of you guys need to consider marrying the single moms in the church and adopting their children as your own. When you do that, do you know what you are? You are a man.

After preaching this text from 1 Timothy, a man in his midfifties approached me with tears in his eyes. He said, "Ted, all morning while you were speaking, I thought about my stepdad. He married my mom and took in all seven of her children and adopted us as his own. He was the greatest man I have ever known." And I agree.

Do you want to be a man of God who puts his faith into practice? If so, take care of widows and orphans: "Religion that God our Father accepts as pure and faultless is this: to look after orphans and widows in their distress and to keep oneself from being polluted by the world" (James 1:27). The best way the church can care for young widows and orphans is to encourage the young single men to marry them and adopt their children.

I remind the young guys at Woodland Hills regularly that we have many single hot mamas at our church. I encourage them to hang out by the children's check-in station and scope them out, then ask them out. No joke. I've even requested that our connection card at Woodland Hills add a couple of check boxes: one box that you can check next to "Single mom, looking for love" and one box next to "Single guy, looking for a hot mama."

Parents may resist the idea of their son marrying a single mom. They may resist because they will suddenly have grandchildren that are not technically theirs, or maybe they resist because their son won't have the American Dream wedding. And the church might encourage the single mom to focus on her kids and not worry about marriage. In either case, please read 1 Timothy 5:1–2, 11–15. *The church is a family.*

You have many moms, dads, brothers, and sisters in the church to help you navigate a blended-family situation. Call on them to guard your young love. Moms, dads, big brothers, and big sisters, don't play the fox to the young love that God asks the church to nurture.

Check out www.youngandinlove.com for video podcasts, articles, and resources to help you prepare for marriage.

Young and in Love Marriage Journal

What aspects of your parents' marriage do you want to model?

Which aspects do you choose to avoid?

How would you define Hollywood's take on dating, love, and marriage? What are some of their most obvious values?

Which cultural values have you embraced as your own?

Fox Alert: Movies

New York Times best-selling author Elizabeth Gilbert wrote the book *Eat Pray Love*. The book begins with Gilbert divorcing her husband in an effort to "discover herself." The book was so popular that they made a movie out of it starring Julia Roberts. In the movie, she visits Italy to eat, India to pray, and Indonesia to love. *USA Today* writer Claudia Puig said of the book and movie that it is a thin story of a "privileged woman who ends her marriage for vague reasons and decides to get in touch with her true self." Puig also added, "The whole journey feels like a rich girl gone slumming."[3] Watch out for foxes on the movie screen. The messages are subtle but influential. More than once I have caught myself watching a movie and saying, "It feels right," when the action or motives in the movie present values that oppose Scripture. Feelings are good and given by God but must be filtered through the Bible.

For further discussion, list a few popular movies you have enjoyed that portray a couple living together or having sex outside of marriage.

Chapter 4

The Consequences

I have been reminded of your sincere faith, which first
lived in your grandmother Lois and in your mother Eunice
and, I am persuaded, now lives in you also.

—2 Timothy 1:5

My generation is the first to get serious about delaying marriage and
family. The median age of first marriages in the 1970s was twenty-
one for women and twenty-three for men. By the year 2009, the
average age for a first marriage climbed to twenty-six for women and
twenty-eight for men.[1]

Born between 1960 and 1980, the Busters are the first generation to stay single for an extended period of time. Our parents, the
Boomers, were the first generation, as a whole, to encourage their
children to delay marriage. Born between 1943 and 1960, the
Boomers thrived on success. Unlike their Builder parents (born

before 1943), the Boomers wanted their children to be successful in everything. For example, the Builders were thrilled their Boomer kids could read. But reading was not good enough for the Boomers' kids. They wanted their kids to read faster. So they bought accelerated reading schedules and enrolled their kids in gifted classes and honors study programs.

Boomers were sent out of the house as adults and were forced to face the cruel, hard world. They heard, "Grow up, get a job, and get married." That expectation came at an early age. But the Boomers delayed the growth of their Buster children and did not send them out so fast. Why? They wanted their kids to succeed. So to guarantee the success of their kids, the Boomer mom and dad protected college and career from all potential evils. Love, marriage, and relationships were the primary distractions from college. So they encouraged their kids to wait, and it worked. For the most part, Busters waited to get established in a career before thinking about marriage and children.

What the Boomers did not realize is that they were unintentionally limiting their own involvement in their future families.

Bye-Bye, Grandma

Grandparents have always been an integral part of family life. Many of us have stories of spending holidays, summer breaks, and vacations with these special people we call Grandma and Grandpa. Eradicating grandparents from our families is just one of the consequences of delaying marriage.

Mark Gungor was the first pastor I heard point out the correlation between delayed marriage, adulthood, and the influence of grandparents. He said, "Those who delay marriage (and subsequently child rearing) are denying themselves one of the greatest joys men and women have cherished for millennia: to participate in the lives of their grandchildren."[2]

Margaret Cadigan was born in 1895. She married my great-grandfather in 1915. They were both twenty years old. They had a child every other year, four children in all. My grandma Mary Jane was their last, born in 1923. Mary Jane waited until she was twenty-four to marry my grandpa Earl. Their delay had just cause. First of all, my grandma did not want to steal the thunder of her sister's wedding. So she told my grandfather they would not get engaged until after her sister's wedding. But her second reason was even stronger. My grandpa served for five years in World War II, a delay you and I probably cannot fathom nowadays.

My grandparents had three daughters. Bonnie married at age twenty, Bev at eighteen, and Jan at nineteen. All three had children early in marriage. Bonnie is my mom, and she had my brother Andy in 1970, a year and a half after her wedding.

Why all the family history? Don't worry, I don't plan to show you pictures of our vacations, but this history is very important. You see, delayed marriage has no roots in history. Delaying marriage is new to my generation, and as a result, couples are having children later. For centuries, couples married young and started families early and this was simply the cultural norm.

Amy and I married early, but we waited seven years to have children. I do not judge people for wanting to delay marriage because of their so-called need to make money, establish a home, jump-start a career, or retain freedom and fun. I wanted that too. I didn't think marriage would stop me, but I believed kids would. Was I selfish? Honestly, in some ways, yes.

Amy and I are the parents of Corynn (born in 2003) and Carson (born in 2005). I was twenty-nine when Corynn was born. If Corynn waits until she is thirty to get married, and then waits five years to have kids, I will be sixty-four when my first grandchild comes on the scene. I'll be sixty-six if Carson follows suit. That's a major shift, considering the fact that my mom became a grandmother at age forty-five when my brother's daughter was born. Do the math. We are only a few generations away from grandparents being removed from the scene altogether. If delayed marriage and having children later continues as a trend, we will systematically remove grandparents from our society.

Not only are we saying bye-bye Grandma, but this phenomenon also has many other consequences.

Delayed Marriage Delays Adulthood

Marriage and family therapist Ryan Pannell defines prolonged adolescence as having too much privilege and not enough responsibility. If you've been handed privilege your entire life, embracing responsibility is difficult. Many permissive, guilt-prone parents felt as though they were damaging their children somehow by asking them to grow up. As a result, parents unintentionally prolonged adolescence and were then stuck with kids who were in no way prepared for adulthood. So some parents pinned their hopes on college or that first job out of high school to help their kids with the growth process.

Marriage comes with great responsibility. You cannot have a successful marriage if you live by the "look out for number one" motto. You always have to consider the feelings and needs of your spouse before making major decisions. And this can be very difficult, especially if you were raised in a kid-centered home in which you ruled the roost. The unnecessary delay of marriage can prolong a sense of entitlement and self-centeredness, which allows some young people to further avoid responsibility. Entitlement carries with it the tone of "I deserve," and it expedites privilege and delays responsibility.

Genesis 2:24 says, "For this reason a man will leave his father and mother and be united to his wife, and they will become one flesh." Marriage happens on the front end of adulthood. This verse establishes marriage as a primary milestone in the life of a young adult, a milestone that marks the transition from childhood to adulthood. The traditional milestones of adulthood include leaving home, getting a job, getting married, and starting a family. God's plan from the very beginning was that you and I would leave home as an adult, not begin a journey to become one.

I'm sad when I meet a seventeen- or eighteen-year-old being raised by parents who have such low expectations for their kids. Maybe your parents gave you too much privilege and no responsibility, but I love you too much to watch you stay under the bondage of low expectations. The reason I believe you can get married at a young age is because I believe you can accept personal responsibility at any age. You don't have to wait to have responsibility handed to you by your parents. You can make the choice today.

The real issue is not your intellect but your maturity and attitude.

I recently ordered a book that I have not yet had the stomach to read. It's called *The Idle Parent: Why Laid-Back Parents Raise Happier and Healthier Kids.* My problem is that I'm not interested in producing happy children, to be really honest with you. I want help raising responsible adults.

You see, I believe that delayed adulthood is the product of overly permissive parenting. As parents, many times we walk in fear of emotionally damaging our kids, so we give them everything they want and make them work for nothing. It gives the child the sense that he or she is in control and, worse, that the world revolves around him or her. That journey should begin and end at home, and if this was your childhood, there's a really simple fix. Become responsible by linking privilege directly to responsibility. Don't use delayed marriage as one more excuse to avoid growing up, because marriage is actually part of the maturing process.

Delayed Marriage Creates Self-Centeredness and Independence

Experts today advocate that delaying marriage gives a person the independence necessary for a strong marriage later. As a pastor, can I share with you frankly? In my office, I have seen it hundreds of times when counseling married couples: One or both spouses share about how they want to live an independent life. *Independent careers. Independent checkbooks. Independent goals. Independent dreams. Even independent churches!* But I see it all the time: The "I'm my own person" attitude is destructive to marriage. That attitude led liberal Gloria Steinem to declare marriage as an arrangement "for one and a half people."

If by independence you mean freedom from responsibility and a few extra years or even a decade for identity exploration, count me out. I appreciate the thoughts of Danielle Crittenden on the identity crisis singles face in our secular culture: "Once a husband and children were thought to be essential to a woman's identity, the sources of purpose in her life; today, they are seen as peripherals, accessories that we attach only after our full identities are up and running."[3]

Independence does not guarantee your character development. Crittenden continued, "By spending years and years living entirely for yourself, thinking only about yourself, and having responsibility to no one but yourself, you end up inadvertently extending the introverted existence of a teenager deep into middle age."[4] I know plenty of guys who work the bare minimum hours at their job, drink way too much, stay up late playing video games and watching porn, and still have some sort of cartoon character on their bedsheets. And they're thirty years old. You see, time alone is not the primary tool of character building. We develop our characters through pain, trials, and difficulty and by how we choose to handle this adversity, not through simple independence. Marriage offers plenty of opportunities to grow our character because it forces us to think about someone other than ourselves.

Fox Alert: Single Friends or Married Friends Who Wish They Were Single

Be careful whom you associate with when you are young and in love. More than likely you have single, immature friends who long to prolong their adolescence—whatever they want to call it. Marriage forces you into a responsibility and selflessness they know nothing about. It may mean finding new friends or associating with different people, which is okay—your time will be limited anyway. And I've seen marriages come to an end when a spouse chooses to live out his or her independence by acting single again. Long nights out with friends on a regular basis are not practical when running a home, raising kids, and working a full-time job.

Delayed Marriage Means Fewer Choices

Branson, Missouri, is a small town, and the single scene is slim pickings. Several years ago I began to meet regularly with Joe, a single drummer in his midtwenties who ultimately moved out of Branson and back to a big city to find love. His motives were good, but his choices here were few.

Young people will switch towns, churches, or schools to find love. Is this the pathetic pursuit of a desperate person? No way! The pursuit of love should be honored by all, especially by church communities. The longer you wait, the slimmer your chances for finding love, according to Danielle Crittenden:

> If a woman remains single until her age creeps up past thirty, she may find herself tapping at her watch and staring down the now mysteriously empty tunnel, wondering if there hasn't been a derailment or accident somewhere along the line. When a train does finally pull in, it is filled with misfits and crazy men—like a New York City subway car after hours; immature, elusive Peter Pans who won't commit themselves to a second cup of coffee, let alone a

second date; neurotic bachelors with strange habits; sexual predators who hit on every woman they meet; newly divorced men taking pleasure wherever they can; embittered, scorned men who still feel vengeful toward their last girlfriend; men who are too preoccupied with their careers to think about anyone else from one week to the next; men who are simply too weak, or odd, to have attracted any other woman's interest. The sensible, decent, not-bad-looking men a woman rejected at twenty-four because she wasn't ready to settle down all seem to have gotten off at other stations.[5]

Delayed marriage is often the result of a delayed search. There's nothing weak or insecure about looking for and desiring a spouse, so make choices early while there are more potential partners to choose from. When foxes begin to chase off the one you've found, think it through seriously.

Fox Alert: College Pastors and Leaders

I know of several residential parachurch ministries that train high school and college graduates. Many of the leaders that run these organizations deter their students from dating in order to focus on studies and their relationship with Christ. Be on guard against any ministry that deters twentysomethings from dating. When you're single and surrounded by hundreds of other singles, that's the perfect time to find someone and get married. If you find yourself in a school or organization that has a policy against dating, you must submit to that authority and honor that policy. But boy oh boy, *you better be looking!*

Delayed Marriage Increases Pressure for Sexual Sin and Increases Your Chances for Divorce

Advocates of delayed marriage believe that delaying marriage increases your chances for a lasting marriage. They say that waiting until you are over the age of twenty-five decreases your chances for divorce.

A study conducted by the National Healthy Marriage Resource Center claimed that postponing marriage until after the age of twenty-five can reduce the chance of divorce by up to 25 percent. The National Center for Health Statistics found nearly half of all marriages in which the bride is eighteen years or younger end in separation or divorce within ten years. For brides twenty-five and older, half as many marriages break up.[6]

However, there's another body of research that delayed marriage advocates leave out. Most research advocating delayed-marriage is conducted by state schools who are not concerned about whether or not their students have sex outside of marriage. So we see that the majority of single people today are delaying marriage but having sex:

> Over 90 percent of American adults experience sex-
> ual intercourse before marrying.... [J]ust under 80
> percent of unmarried, church-going, conservative

Protestants who are currently dating someone are having sex of some sort.[7]

Premarital sex and/or living together prior to marriage (cohabitation) increase your chances of divorce considerably. Sex in marriage is too wonderful to allow it to be a fox before marriage.

Delayed Marriage Declares Singleness as Normative and Ideal

Singleness is a touchy subject in the church. Scripture can be twisted and used in whatever way necessary, depending on the point you are trying to make. You can point to 1 Corinthians 7, where Paul says that it is "good for them to stay unmarried" (v. 8) and that "those who marry will face many troubles in this life, and I want to spare you this" (v. 28). But God said that everything He created was good. The only thing that was "not good" was man being alone. In Genesis 2 it says, "The LORD God said, 'It is not good for the man to be alone. I will make a helper suitable for him'" (v. 18). Solomon told us to "enjoy life with your wife, whom you love" (Eccl. 9:9). And Proverbs notes, "He who finds a wife finds what is good and receives favor from the LORD" (18:22). So which verse do we follow? Which do we throw out? The answer is simple. Don't throw out any of them. Keep and follow all of them.

I had the opportunity to speak this past summer to all of the missionary candidates for a major church denomination. I've spoken to the married missionaries in years past, but this time they asked me to consider speaking to a joint session of both couples and singles. The couples from previous years felt that the sessions I taught on marriage would be beneficial to single people as well.

So I delivered my favorite marriage talk out of Ecclesiastes, which I call, "Cheer up, you'll soon be dead." The outline of the talk is simple: Life is hard. Then you die. But in the meantime, enjoy life with your wife (Eccl. 9:7–9). We always have a lot of fun in that session, but this particular time, there was one young man who would have none of it.

At the end of my session he came down front and asked if he could say a few words. Since I was an invited guest, it wasn't up to me. I handed him my microphone, and he was off to the races. In a nutshell, here's what he said: "I am tired of people in the church making marriage out to be the greatest thing ever. It is demeaning to singles."

He went on for about ten minutes and validated nearly every point I had just made on prolonged adolescence. When I got the microphone back, I didn't come down on him but gently said, "Paul made it very clear that the ability to stay single and celibate is for the few who can exercise self-control. For most of us men, sex is something we have a deep desire for on a regular basis. If you can live a life free of sex and masturbation and faithfully serve the Lord, then you are the exception, not the rule. For the rest of us, we must marry."

I made it my goal to befriend this young man before I left. One thing I've learned from hanging around older, wiser men is that people who are hurting often hurt other people. The issue is rarely ever the issue. This young, single missionary was frustrated after being turned down for financial support from churches simply because he was single. That's an entirely different issue, and I can validate his hurt, but nonetheless we must promote and honor marriage.

Pastor Mark Driscoll of Mars Hill Seattle wrote, "Indeed, single-ness is not bad, as exemplified by Jeremiah, Jesus, and Paul. Still, singleness is neither normative nor superior to marriage."[8] We cannot elevate singleness above marriage; rather, we should advocate for marriage over singleness. It prevents sin and honors God's plan for His people.

Fox Alert: A Bad Interpretation of 1 Corinthians 7:6-9

Be careful not to use this passage in 1 Corinthians as an excuse to delay marriage for a vocation in ministry or a place of service in the church. Singleness is the exception, not the rule. If you have maintained self-control over lust and masturbation, then you may be one of Paul's concessions.

Delayed Marriage Could Eventually Mean No Marriage At All
    Newsweek magazine recently developed a series of articles called "Marriage Reconsidered." One of the articles in the series was called "I Don't: The Case Against Marriage." Writers Jessica Bennett and Jesse Ellison are "modern" women with a postmodern take on marriage:

> Once upon a time, marriage made sense. It was
> how women ensured their financial security, got
> the fathers of their children to stick around, and
> gained access to a host of legal rights. But 40 years

after the feminist movement established our rights in the workplace, a generation after the divorce rate peaked, and a decade after *Sex and the City* made singledom chic, marriage is—from a legal and practical standpoint, anyway—no longer necessary.... Women now constitute a majority of the workforce; we're more educated, less religious, and living longer, with vacuum cleaners and washing machines to make domestic life easier. We're also the breadwinners (or co-breadwinners) in two thirds of American families.... We have our own health care and 401(k)s and no longer need a marriage license to visit our partners in the hospital. For many of us, marriage doesn't even mean a tax break.[9]

For some the delay is indefinite. They weigh the decision to marry in the same balance as 401(k) contributions, health plans, taxes, and education. I argue that to do so dishonors marriage. Marriage and family still make sense because they are a higher calling than your job, education, or location.

Responding to the musings of this article, Dr. Albert Mohler, president of Southern Baptist Theological Seminary, wrote:

The essay by Jessica Bennett and Jesse Ellison is an undeniable reminder of our challenge to rebuild a marriage culture, and to start inside our own churches. "Once upon a time, marriage made sense," Bennett and Ellison assert. One essential task for the Christian Church is to rebuild and maintain a marriage culture—even when marriage itself no longer makes sense to so many around us.[10]

As the world moves away from marriage, I feel an increased urgency and see even more reason for young people to embrace the Bible, get married, and start a family. Fighting battles on the courthouse steps over gay marriage is not the solution. Rather, getting married and staying faithful to your spouse is the only solution. When we get a few million Jesus followers modeling the gospel in their marriages, we will see a revolution sweep the world.

Days before completing this manuscript, I saw the November 2010 cover story of *Time* magazine, which read, "Who Needs Marriage?" The article was written in response to the engagement of Prince William and Kate Middleton. Their on-again, off-again relationship left many wondering if this "modern" couple would *ever* get married, and their 2011 wedding will surely ignite many spirited conversations.

This book challenges the unnecessary delay of marriage, but I'm afraid we have a bigger battle on our hands. According to the *Time* magazine article, 39 percent of Americans believe that marriage is becoming obsolete. A *Time*/Pew poll found that 44 percent of Americans under thirty believe marriage is "heading for extinction."[11] Apparently, some think that delayed marriage is just a stop along the way to wiping marriage out altogether.

Check out www.youngandinlove.com for video podcasts,
articles, and resources to help you prepare for marriage.

Young and in Love Marriage Journal

*What are your top three reasons for delaying marriage?
What would be the consequences of that decision?*

*If you marry early, do you plan on delaying children?
If so, why?*

*List some examples of independence turning into
selfishness.*

How can independence break down a marriage?

Why is marriage normative for the believer?

Fox Alert: The "Look Out for Number One" Attitude

Pride and selfishness destroy marriage. We see it displayed in the lives
of everyone from movie stars and rock stars to our neighbors next
door. If you've ever watched the television "soap drama" *Desperate
Housewives,* then you've seen attitude. This self-centered chorus in
our culture goes beyond natural concern for one's health, welfare,
and future and turns into a self-obsession. With a naval-gazing,

me-centric focus, it's impossible to know what it means to be in a loving relationship with God, let alone with others, such as one's spouse. The result is only hollow satisfaction. Jesus said that if you try to keep your life for yourself, you will lose it (Luke 17:33). Only by losing your life and giving it up to God can you find abundant life.

Chapter 5

Necessary Delays

Take me away with you—let us hurry! Let the
king bring me into his chambers.

—Song of Songs 1:4

Three thousand years ago people called bedrooms "chambers." When love grows, as we see in Song of Songs, desire tends to rush things. But there's a difference between a rushed marriage and a young marriage. A twenty-three-year-old friend of mine recently shared the news of his engagement after eighteen months of dating his girlfriend. The first person to respond to his engagement announcement asked him, "What's the rush?"

Are you kidding me? It was seventeen months from the night I first met Amy to the day of our wedding. We would have been married within a year if it hadn't been for the traditional wedding we felt the pressure to plan. Fourteen years later, Amy and I both agree that we should have married right after graduation, twelve months after we met.

Discovering the differences between necessary and unnecessary delays will help you keep from rushing into a bad marriage and at the same time remove the obstacles to setting a wedding date. The foxes in your life can sometimes blur the line between necessary and unnecessary delays. But I encourage you to *chase those foxes away!*

What's the Rush?

If you're not careful, you may jump into marriage with haste. The buds of young love require a season to mature. You need this season to inspect the character of the one you will commit your life to. However, if you need years to do so, then I'd say you are a horrible investigator. Recruit your friends and family to help you make a discerning decision and avoid unnecessary delays.

There are a few "rushes" to ponder before heading to the court-house to pick up a marriage license. As you read through these rushes, please keep in mind that all marriages require commitment, fidelity, and responsibility. Rushing past those markers in an effort to cover up sin, save a few bucks, or just to have sex is never a good idea.

The Pregnancy Rush

One night of sex does not make a marriage. While raising children in a home with both the mother and the father is ideal, it is not required. If the father or mother of your child is not a follower of Jesus, I do not recommend getting married. Marriage only works with character and commitment. Do not rush into marriage because you are expecting; rather, go through the process of pastoral counseling and get the support of your church and family.

The Military Rush

I've had the opportunity to help integrate soldiers back into their families, churches, and communities after returning home from war. Due to basic training and deployment, a couple might get married to secure benefits for the spouse of the soldier. Money and benefits are never good reasons to rush into something as serious as marriage. If an early deployment date means rushing past a season of character inspection, you must wait.

The Relocation Rush

Amy and I spent the time of our engagement over a thousand miles apart. It was hard, and at the time it felt very unnecessary—but it was only for five months. Sometimes a job will require relocation before a ceremony can be had. It's always better to spend a few extra bucks to live apart for a season and later marry well.

The Escape-Home Rush

Leaving a bad home environment is not a good reason to rush marriage. When this happens, both the young man and young woman are in danger of exiting one bad situation and entering into another.

The Ceremony Rush

The wedding day itself can force either a rush or a delay. Some rush into marriage because they've been dreaming of the big day for years. They are more in love with the idea of the wedding than they are in love with their would-be spouse. The church is far more concerned about your marriage.

The Savings Rush

This is often the reason people rush into marriage and is one of the primary excuses for cohabitation. Combining your incomes and decreasing your expenses makes sense, especially during a difficult economy. During this recession I've had to talk a lot of couples out of cohabitating in an attempt to save a few dollars.

The Sex Rush

Comedian Jeff Foxworthy says, "Getting married for sex is like buying a 747 for the free peanuts." Is sex a valid reason to marry? Yes. Should it be the primary reason? No. Is sex ever a reason to rush? Absolutely not! Remember, God's plan is delay sex, get married, then enjoy sex. The world says, "Go ahead and have sex whenever and with whomever you want." As Christians, we believe that marriage is where one man and one woman enjoy each other for a lifetime.

Every bud of love has a season. If the bud does not eventually bloom, it dries up and falls to the ground. When I meet couples who've been dating for five or more years I am always shocked. *How in the world have you been able to do that?* is my first thought. I immediately assume they are involved sexually or that the guy is masturbating regularly. So what's a healthy length of time for delay?

I knew I wanted to marry Amy on the night I met her. We dated for a year and were engaged for just over five months. Once the decision to marry has been made, I encourage couples to think in terms of months, not years. You do not need to date for two more years to see if you're compatible or to plan a posh wedding. Long delays are unnecessary. But some delays are absolutely necessary and need to be accepted.

The High School Delay

I do not encourage couples to marry in high school. I'm not some freaky cult preacher who wants to move to the middle of nowhere and marry off all the young women in the church. But I have blessed some eighteen-year-old high school graduates to marry. It is rare, but every now and then I meet a young person who went from childhood to adulthood in their early teens and matured very quickly. That was the case with TJ and Shannon. As college freshmen, they asked if I would be willing to do their premarital counseling. At first I was hesitant because TJ still looked like a *high school freshman*.

Then I heard TJ's story.

TJ lost his dad at an early age and took responsibility for his younger siblings in his early teens. He accepted this responsibility and worked to provide for his family. In our first session together, he shared gut-wrenching stories of the pain and trials he'd endured in his young life. I was in awe of his maturity and of the bold way he stepped up to help his family. It made perfect sense that he settled on College of the Ozarks here in Missouri. The college's slogan is "Hard Work U." Each student attends the college tuition-free in exchange for fifteen hours of work a week on campus alongside their school load and any other job they may hold down to pay the bills. TJ even shared about his job with great enthusiasm.

By the time TJ finished sharing his story, I was ready to graduate them and set the date for their wedding. He was wise beyond his years. I still hadn't heard about his love for Shannon, but I thought to myself, *This guy will make a fantastic husband! He is full of life, loves Jesus, and is an adult.* After our meeting—and remember that this is a rare situation—I enthusiastically applauded their young love and told these recent high school graduates to "set the date."

My friend Joe White has been leading summer sports camps in Branson for forty years. Joe regularly speaks to teens at an event he calls "Pure Excitement." He often reminds young people of the statistic that only 2 percent of high school students marry someone they dated in high school. Good reminder for those young high school students who think they have found "the one."

But let's say you are in that 2 percent—what should you do?

First of all, you are not weird. Rare, but not weird! If you feel you've found the guy or gal you want to marry and you're still in high school, then you need to move forward on a few things with great tenacity. First of all, make sure you grow up and leave your adolescence behind. Start showing your family and friends that you can take on added responsibility.

Second, honor your parents and their discernment. You are not a legal adult until the age of eighteen (sixteen in some states), and your parents get the final say. If you show them an attitude and whine about it, then you're still an adolescent and not ready to marry anyway.

Third, if you want to marry after high school I would encourage you to get a job. Start saving your money now while you're at home and expenses are low. Go work somewhere thirty or more hours a week somewhere to gain experience, training, and responsibility.

The Christ-Follower Delay

More than a delay, marrying someone who doesn't follow Jesus is a "don't." This delay is not only necessary but also a biblical mandate. The primary caution here is that a guy or gal may stage a Jesus experience just so you can get married. Faith in Jesus is a start, but the fruit of his or her decision needs to be hanging on the tree.

Willingly going into a marriage knowing that your spouse does not profess Jesus Christ as his or her Lord and Savior is prohibited in the Bible. In 2 Corinthians 6, Paul said, "Do not be yoked together with unbelievers. For what do righteousness and wickedness have in common? Or what fellowship can light have with darkness? What harmony is there between Christ and Belial? What does a believer have in common with an unbeliever?" (vv. 14–15).

The reference here to a yoke comes from Deuteronomy 22:10. The yoke is a farming tool placed over the heads of animals and attached to an implement used to work a field. In Deuteronomy, the children of Israel were commanded not to yoke an ox and a donkey. The ox was a clean animal, but the donkey was not. These animals also possessed entirely different levels of strength and pulled at different paces. This made for an unclean and awkward team. The same thing happens in a marriage when a husband and wife are processing life through opposite worldviews. This mismatch affects everything: raising kids, paying bills, spending money, attending church, and caring for aging parents.

There's an old-school term that was coined way back in the twentieth century called "missionary dating." A Christian would fall in love with a non-Christian and share Jesus with him or her until he or she believed in Him too. I had many non-Christian friends who started following

Christ because they fell for a young woman in our youth group. They might attend a weekend retreat or summer camp just to enjoy the six-hour van ride with this young woman. Not a lot of discipling going on there!

Ladies, be warned. At Woodland Hills Family Church we minister weekly to countless wives attending our church alone. They married a guy with a marginal faith or no faith at all. Many were "not equally yoked" from the start of their marriages. Now they attend church alone, frustrated and desiring more. To keep from becoming jaded they need to be encouraged with 1 Peter 3:1–6. They can pray for their husband, Christ can do a work in his heart, and some can find hope in an unequally yoked marriage. But I'm not talking to those women right now. It's a blessing to talk to you before you make that mistake yourself. Do not marry an unbeliever or someone who professes Christ but shows no fruit. Marry that young man (or young woman) who understands that he must deny himself daily, pick up his cross, and follow Christ.

Character is the first of four Cs we will cover in a couple of chapters. A secure, maturing faith is the foundation for character. If you are smitten with love, and he is an unbeliever, be strong and break up with him at once. If you are attracted and thinking about marriage with a young woman who does not know Jesus, be a man, and with a Christlike spirit, end the relationship.

Fox Alert: New Believer

Are you dating and considering marriage with someone who is a brand-new Christian? That person needs to experience a season of discipleship and testing. The same is true in church leadership; Paul encouraged young Timothy to "not be hasty" (1 Tim. 5:22) in installing new elders or to make sure that they are not "recent convert[s]" (1 Tim. 3:6).

I've always been a little freaked out by men and women who convert to a religion in order to get married or in some instances just to have a wedding in a particular church, temple, or synagogue. Bad idea! Be cautious of the young man or woman who "converts" to Christianity just to please you or your parents.

The Parent Delay

Above all else, honor your parents by involving them in your decision to marry. Dishonoring Mom and Dad in this decision is ultimately dishonoring the Lord. Solomon did not wear a royal crown to his wedding, even though he was a king. Instead, he wore a crown his mother gave him as a sign of her blessing:

> Come out, you daughters of Zion,
> and look at King Solomon wearing the crown,
> the crown with which his mother crowned him
> on the day of his wedding,
> the day his heart rejoiced. (Song 3:11)

You become a legal adult at eighteen with the right to marry anyone you like without your parents' permission. But the crown of your parents' blessing honors your decision and blesses them in return. So go for the crown of your parents' blessing!

In all of human history, asking Amy's dad for his blessing was the easiest "ask" on record. I woke up in the guest room of their home early one June morning in 1996. While I got dressed, I was psyching myself up to make it the very first conversation at the breakfast table. Everyone knew it was coming, so I didn't want a big pink elephant joining us for the meal.

I marched down the stairs to ask Mr. Freitag for his daughter's hand. What happened next caught me by complete surprise.

"Good morning, Mr. Freitag, how are you?" I asked.

"Well, Ted, I hate my job, but I guess most people do," he answered abruptly. How do you respond to that? Apparently, he had a bad time at work the day prior and was not looking forward to returning. I decided to wait until after breakfast.

We were standing together in the kitchen after breakfast when I popped the question.

"Mr. Freitag, I would like to ask your daughter to marry me, and—" I began but was quickly interrupted.

In his thick Norwegian accent he said, "You betcha, Ted!"

And that was that. We were done.

I was prepared to say, "Mr. Freitag, I would like to ask your daughter to marry me, and I was wondering if you had a few minutes to talk?" I spent all morning *wordsmithing* that line. But it wasn't needed.

Your parents will probably be the greatest voice of influence in your decision to delay marriage. Every parent has milestones, spoken and unspoken, that they want to see their children hit before they marry. Your parents' fear of your young marriage may be directly linked to how well they did with teaching you responsibility and balancing it with privilege. Most parents I know today see college or trade school as a last chance to try to ensure their children's success. To keep you on pace with those milestones they may turn to threats like "I won't pay for college" or "I won't pay for the wedding."

These milestones are not the only reasons parents advocate delay and withhold their blessing. Here are a few more reasons your parents may encourage you to wait:

> **Fear of failure**: Maybe your parents believe they haven't prepared you well. They do not want their failure to translate into the failure of your future marriage and a possible divorce.
>
> **Discerning certain qualities in your choice**: Don't overlook the possibility that you may have made a poor choice in a spouse. Parents generally have great radar, so lean on it.
>
> **They don't want you to miss out**: If your parents married early, they may encourage you to wait because of what they feel they missed out on. They may even tell you, "You have the rest of your life to be married; take the time now to enjoy yourself."
>
> **You were in love once before and had a bad breakup, and they don't want that pain for you again**: They may interpret your love as the kind of puppy love that you may have experienced in high school.
>
> **Cultural taboos**: They may want you to go with the flow and keep up with the Joneses. They have placed marriage at the end of the spectrum of adulthood milestones. Success in their mind might mean that you get into a good college, find a

good job, and *then* get married. It's a socially acceptable order
of events.

Selfishness: They want to keep you at home to satisfy their
personal desires or needs. Single parents can fall into this
trap.

They're not emotionally prepared: They may be dreading
the empty-nest years and may not feel ready.

They're not financially prepared: They may not be ready
to pay for the wedding. You can ease this by adjusting your
expectations of their involvement.

Ultimately, you want the crown of your parents' blessing
because it recognizes and honors their role in your life. They
raised you, fed you, schooled you, and clothed you, and you must
honor their hard work. While they need to acknowledge your
rite of passage into adulthood, you need to praise them for their
investment in you. You're leaving home as an adult and beginning
your own home, your own family. You are no longer a child, and
you want to leave home in a way that says, "Thank you, Mom and
Dad." Never use the words, "I'm an adult—I'll do what I want."
Those words spring only from the mouth of an adolescent.

The crown is not always possible. If you can't get their blessing, you still need to honor your parents and esteem them and
their feelings as highly valuable. You can honor them without
agreeing with them. Your skill in doing so will help you as a
spouse. You will spend much of your married life honoring your
spouse even though you do not agree with him or her. That's the
recipe for success in every area of life.

Respect for Authority Begins at Home

No matter what kind of parents you grew up with, whether they were dominant, permissive, or neglectful (or loving and fun!), your ability to deal with authority is determined largely by how you processed the authority of your own mom and dad. I know that some young people think that parents sit up at night, thinking up evil schemes for the next day just to keep their kids from being happy. However, your mom and dad are your authority, not your archenemies.

How we relate to our parents affects every other relationship in our lives. When we are young, we learn to obey our parents. This lasts only for a short period of time—eighteen years or so. But after that, we will spend a lifetime honoring and blessing them. By obeying our mom and dad when we are young, we learn important skills for life. But none of us are with our parents forever. They're a part of our training that God places in our lives to help us become well-rounded and well-adjusted adults.

Ephesians 6:1–3 says, "Children, obey your parents in the Lord, for this is right. 'Honor your father and mother'—which is the first commandment with a promise—'that it may go well with you and that you may enjoy long life on the earth.'" "Obey your parents in the Lord" essentially means that you are to obey your mom and dad as though you were obeying the Lord. Even if your parents are not believers, you must honor and obey them, unless they command you to be sinful in some way.

When you're young and living at home, you are commanded to obey your parents. The transition from childhood to adulthood alters the way we relate to our parents. As adults, we do not obey our parents. We no longer call them to find out what our next move in life should be. We no longer ask them for permission to take a vacation or a trip. But we do honor them. Again, *honor* means to esteem as highly valuable. Involving your parents in the decision to marry is not an issue of obedience but an issue of honor.

According to the Scripture, your relationship with your parents changes when you leave home (Gen. 2:24). Hopefully you are leaving home earlier than many of the young people in our culture, who are now waiting until their mid- to late twenties to leave home. Whenever this happens for you, there is a relationship change. You disconnect from that bond you had with your parents when you were a child, but the requirement to honor them still remains.

God takes honor so seriously that He gives some strong words to the young man or woman who would dishonor their parents:

> Children who mistreat their father or chase away their
>   mother are an embarrassment and a public disgrace.
>   (Prov. 19:26 NLT)

> The eye that mocks a father,
>   that scorns obedience to a mother,
>   will be pecked out by the ravens of the valley,
>   will be eaten by the vultures. (Prov. 30:17)

We honor our mom and dad when we tell them thank you for teaching us right from wrong. Let your parents off the hook if you have a bone to pick with them. Your mom and dad worried about you, spent time with you, and spent hard-earned money to raise you.

In some cases, your parents taught you God's Word and prayed for you.

So when you get together with them, don't focus on all the imperfections and everything they did wrong. Focus on the teachings they tried their best to give you because they knew it was right.

Nothing says thank you to parents more than young people who acknowledge what they were taught as children:

> Listen, my son, to your father's instruction
>   and do not forsake your mother's teaching.
> They will be a garland to grace your head
>   and a chain to adorn your neck. (Prov. 1:8–9)

Show Your Parents You're Ready to Marry

When your relationship moves toward marriage, it will probably come as no surprise to your parents. Even if they love and respect the one you plan to marry, you still need to go for the crown by having the guy officially ask the father of the bride for his daughter's hand. This is old school, I know.

The following questions will help you ask for the parents' blessing. Answer these twenty questions *before* you make the approach. Use the questions to help you write a letter, prepare a speech, or work through a dialogue.

> Define love.
> How will you love her as much as her dad does?
> How will you resolve conflict?

Where will you serve in the church?

What did your parents teach you about marriage?

What did your parents teach you about how to treat a
young woman?

How do you honor your folks? Give some practical
examples.

Who is the most influential leader in your life, and
why?

Do you regularly expose yourself to sexually explicit
material?

What steps have you taken to keep yourself pure?

Are you sexually addicted or struggling with
pornography?

When did you become a follower of Jesus?

What would keep you from following Christ?

What are your favorite hobbies or sports?

What are you sacrificing for this marriage?

How did the two of you meet?

What was your first impression of the young woman
you hope to marry?

When did you know she was the one?

Would you consider yourself a great listener?

How will you make a living in the next five years?

Ladies, this list and approach come with a caution. If your boyfriend or fiancé has a serious reaction to answering these questions
or approaching your dad, he's not ready to get married. I'm not saying, "Don't marry him." I am saying, "Don't marry him right now."

He might need some more work on his character and his ability to submit to authority.

Check out www.youngandinlove.com for video podcasts, articles, and resources to help you prepare for marriage.

Young and in Love Marriage Journal

What are some practical ways you can honor your parents?

How have you observed your boyfriend, girlfriend, or fiancé(e) honor his or her parents?

What will be the challenges you will face in asking for your parents' blessing?

How will you approach these challenges?

If your parents do not approve, how will you honor them?

How can you still honor parents even when they say no?

If you met in high school, what have you done to prepare for marriage at a very young age?

Briefly share your salvation experience.

Fox Alert: Single Parents

Jaded single parents sometimes pose a serious threat to young love. Such parents make two mistakes. First, they assume that their child's marriage will go down the same path as their own. Second, the single parent can be selfish and struggle with relinquishing time with their child. A mom or dad who has unresolved anger, bitterness, or resentment toward his or her ex can write negative and often false beliefs about marriage onto a child's heart. Do not allow a bitter parent to keep you from or interfere with your young marriage.

However, there are several benefits and blessings when you include your parents in the marriage decision-making process.

First of all, it shows them that you appreciate them, and this pleases God. He favors adult children who appreciate and take care of their parents. Paul in 1 Timothy 5 said that providing for our parents to repay them is "pleasing to God" (v. 4). God is honored when we honor our parents.

Second, it gives your soon-to-be husband or wife a good and welcomed start in your family. I'm assuming that you plan on visiting family for holidays and special events. A nod of approval from Mom and Dad makes for lighter and more relaxing turkey dinners.

Third, parents can offer another discerning voice. Estrogen and testosterone are bad stand-alone decision makers. Mom and/or Dad are two more voices in the screening process.

Chapter 6

Unnecessary Delays

Happy marriages begin when we marry the ones we love,
and they blossom when we love the ones we marry.

—Tom Mullen

Frequent weddings are part of a healthy church. No weddings means either bad teaching or no new people coming into the church. As a pastor, I am responsible for teaching sound doctrine; growth is God's part and a direct result of sound doctrine (Acts 2:47). While most of my teaching is from the front on Sunday mornings, I also get to teach a lot when I am with young couples. Most of the time, I'm on defense.

Most sessions feel like I'm reading from a frequently-asked-questions page on a website. Young couples will ask a boilerplate question, and I give a biblical response. I usually start each premarital session with a little humor by saying, "My job is to see if I can keep the two of you from marrying." That usually breaks the ice. Sometimes they interpret my joke as meaning I'm just one more person who wants to stifle their love.

I take my job as pastor very seriously because Scripture makes it clear that I am doubly responsible for the advice I give (Heb. 13:17). Much of my premarital counseling consists of simply removing the obstacles of unnecessary delay.

The Spreadsheet Delay

At a recent marriage conference I conducted in Oklahoma City, I met a sharp young guy decked out all in red. He could have been the Oklahoma University mascot. No joke, he had the school logo on every piece of clothing he wore, down to his keychain. Standing next to him was a stunning young woman with a smile that said, *We're happily married.* But they were not. They were happy but not yet married.

I asked my boilerplate question: "How long have you two been dating?"

"Six years," she replied.

"Six years!" I gasped as I turned my attention toward the mascot. "Dude, what's the problem?"

"I know, I know, you hit the nail on the head in the last talk, even down to our age," he said. "I'm twenty-eight, and she's twenty-six."

"Go ahead, honey. Tell him why we're not married," she insisted.

Now I must admit that they were a great couple who kept things lighthearted and really seemed to enjoy each other.

"Well, I'm a ... " he started, but she finished with, "He's an accountant, and he has several financial goals he would like to meet before we get married."

"Please tell me you don't have a spreadsheet for this marriage and your wedding," I guessed.

He smiled.

"You're seriously waiting until the spreadsheet gives you the nod?" I asked him. Then I turned my questioning to her. "You are a saint—why are you waiting for this accountant to balance his spreadsheet?"

Professor Mark Regnerus addressed this issue: "Marrying young can spell poverty, at least temporarily.... Good marriages grow through struggles, including economic ones."[1]

Let me interpret that for you. Think egg-crate furniture and a mattress on the floor, not Ethan Allen or Posturepedic. Think top ramen or spaghetti at home for dinner most nights, not Applebee's. Grab Folgers on the way out the door in the morning, not Starbucks on the way to work.

Countless young couples call our church office every year, asking for marriage counseling. Ryan Pannell is a licensed marriage and family therapist and ordained minister in our church. He does not receive a salary from the church, so we charge a small fee to couples who meet with him. I do my best to keep his schedule full because he's very good at what he does, but also because it frees me up to devote myself "to the public reading of Scripture, to preaching and to teaching" (1 Tim. 4:13).

My assistant, Denise Bevins, keeps my calendar and schedules all of my appointments. She regularly sends people to Ryan, and they are blessed all the more for spending time with him. But sometimes she gets pushback from the couples: "We can't afford it; we need to meet with Ted." If the couple makes it through Denise's screening, then I'll meet with them.

When they show up with their venti Frappuccinos from Starbucks and set them on the table in front of me, my eyes fixate on those clear plastic cups with a drizzle of chocolate atop a mountain of whipped cream. It infuriates me. Ryan's fee is the price of six or so of those drinks. You can imagine why couples are stunned when part of Denise's screening for counseling includes this final question: "When was the last time you bought a drink from Starbucks?" Marriage is far more affordable than you may think. Give me a couple of minutes with your weekly budget and I'll show you.

Modern entitlement makes us want things now, things our parents might have spent thirty years accumulating. It is unnecessary to delay marriage just to maintain an absurd standard of living, and you can avoid the spreadsheet delay by adjusting your lifestyle, having realistic expectations, and working hard. If you can't make it working forty hours per week, then start thinking about overtime or a second job.

Fox Alert: Money

The love of money can destroy your marriage. Young couples have a tendency to become slaves to debt and end up lovers of money and haters of each other. Avoid borrowing whenever possible: "The rich rule over the poor, and the borrower is servant to the lender" (Prov. 22:7). Make sure that your use of credit does not replace your trust in God's timing: "Be still before the LORD and wait patiently for him; do not fret when men succeed in their ways, when they carry out their wicked schemes" (Ps. 37:7). Avoid using credit when buying things you want, not things you need, and be content: "But godliness with contentment is great gain. For we brought nothing into the world, and we can take nothing out of it. But if we have food and clothing, we will be content with that" (1 Tim. 6:6–8). And pay your debts on time, for "the wicked borrow and do not repay, but the righteous give generously" (Ps. 37:21).

The Education Delay

This is the most common delay.

I married Amy in 1996, between her junior and senior years at Liberty University. We thought about delaying a year to let her finish her senior year on campus, but that was too long for both of us to wait. Instead, we had the blessing of Liberty's extended-learning program, and Amy was able to finish her degree through correspondence.

There are several reasons why the education delay is unnecessary.

First of all, college is not for everyone, but it's become a milestone of success in our country. Parents treat it as the last effort in securing their child's future. It is now assumed that every high school graduate will head off to college. But the fact is, some young people spend a year or two in college and decide it's not for them. And that is okay. Men and women alike can choose occupations that do not require college degrees.

Second, and I know this is a crazy thought, but what about expediting your marriage and delaying college? What? You may be thinking: *Heretic! This guy's a false teacher.* But the fact remains that mature twentysomething adults can be married while attending college. I have a dear family friend who recently completed college in his thirties. He has been very successful and has a fantastic family. I know others who have gotten married while in college and completed their studies while young and poor and working. It can be done.

Third, this delay can mean loss of cash, because, as I said, some parents will discontinue tuition assistance if you marry prior to graduation. Amy and I took this as a challenge. It felt chivalrous to be able to tell Amy's parents that I was excited to pay for her senior year of college.

The Job Delay

This is probably the second most common delay, and it often makes sense to the majority of young people. After all, they did not set up the American Dream, but for some reason, many of them feel they must conform to it. But it doesn't have to work that way:

> Fifty years ago ... a woman didn't need to ... "live on her own" to get to know herself. Today, a young woman needs to graduate college, perhaps get some grad school, and try a few jobs.... Once she has established her own merits—her own self-worth—she's ready to shop for a husband;

she might be 30 by then. Did she delay marriage? Hardly. She was racing through society's hurdles as fast as she could.[2]

When you're just getting started in marriage, things are extremely tight. It's hard, and you must chase entitlement from your home. Entitlement says, "I deserve." Entitlement sets unrealistic expectations for income and lifestyle; it cops an attitude toward authority because you always feel like you're worth more than you are. Don't miss the common denominator here: *you*.

Maybe you're considering delaying marriage until you land the perfect job or climb the ladder at your current place of work. I say it doesn't matter—work a job that may not be perfect, but one that pays the bills. I had more than one job I despised early in our marriage, but all along I was thrilled to care for Amy. Also, being married young was great because I loved coming home and telling Amy that the company I worked for gave me a promotion or a generous Christmas bonus. I always enjoyed giving Amy the "extra" money that came in.

Fox Alert: The American Dream

Most parents want their kids to graduate from college and get a good job. The American Dream says you can be whomever you want to be and do whatever you want to do. This is bad advice for the follower of Christ! Instead, start by asking the question, "What has the Lord shaped me to be?" You are His masterpiece, and He has plans for you (Eph. 2:10). College may or may not be a part of that plan. A job with a huge salary may or may not be a part of that plan. Young marriage may be.

The Ceremony Delay

If money's tight, it's absolutely ridiculous to delay a marriage for a posh wedding ceremony. Delaying marriage until you can afford a wedding with all the trimmings is unnecessary. Less is more.

During the writing of this book, Chelsea Clinton got married in Rhinebeck, New York. The wedding of the daughter of former president Bill Clinton and Secretary of State Hillary Clinton was the lead story on every newscast. The bill for the wedding was estimated between two and three million dollars. That's six thousand dollars per person in attendance. Nice. But it got me thinking. The average wedding in our country costs twenty thousand dollars. What if I told you that six thousand dollars total could give you a storybook wedding? What, you don't believe me?

I've officiated weddings ranging in cost from a few hundred dollars to the high six figures. I've performed ceremonies under large tents, in gardens, on rocky bluffs, and in castles, chapels, and churches. I've stood before intimate gatherings of twenty guests and sprawling events for five hundred guests. But the wedding my wife and I keep talking about took place at our favorite resort in southwest Missouri. Johnny Morris, the founder of Bass Pro Shops, built Big Cedar. Now, before you guess that our favorite wedding included a bunch of rednecks at a marina with strings of shotgun-shell lights, you need to know that Big Cedar is a luxurious resort and spa in a woodland setting. It's the wedding we've dreamed about for our daughter. But, of course, she'll have to have her say.

The wedding ceremony took place at sunset. The bride and groom hailed from opposite ends of the country and traveled to Branson with only their immediate families. Big Cedar sits on Table Rock Lake with several dozen cabins and lodges lining the shore. This particular wedding took place on a point with a 180-degree view of the water. It was gorgeous.

Amy and I walked into this quaint cabin and were greeted by twenty to thirty people laughing and having a good time. We mingled for thirty minutes or so before I accompanied the bride and groom out onto the balcony just before sunset. I stood with my back up against the balcony. The bride and groom faced each other, holding hands, and the best man and maid of honor stood by their sides. And through the double doors stood their family and my precious bride, Amy. The sunset painted our backdrop. They exchanged vows and rings and stepped inside for a few photos, cake, and punch. It was relaxed, picturesque, tear-filled, and over-the-top memorable. Cost?

Weekend for family at Big Cedar:	$1,700
Wedding Dress:	$500
Wedding to Remember:	Priceless

Consider cheaper weddings. I love being a part of destination weddings, beach weddings, family backyard weddings, after-Sunday-morning-service weddings, casual weddings, theme weddings, and, dare I say it, *elopement*. Yes, elopement is perfectly legal, but make

sure your elopement honors your parents. Sarah Palin and her husband, Todd, met in high school and married soon after in 1988,
and they eloped to avoid the high cost of a wedding. After a rough
year of fishing, their money was tight. Their wedding cost thirty-five
dollars.[3]

There are a few simple guidelines to consider as you plan your
wedding and avoid unnecessary delay. Don't allow your parents to tap
into their home equity line of credit to pay for your wedding. Dave
Ramsey would call that "Stupid!" You can help your parents pay for
the wedding. Shoot, you can even offer to pay for the whole thing!
Mom and dad of bride do not have to pay for your over-the-top
dream wedding. Face it—some traditions may need to die to expe-
dite your marriage. When you approach your parents, come up with
a plan rooted in the philosophy "Less is more." Consider better alter-
natives to big, expensive weddings. Go on a short, close-to-home
honeymoon. Save your money and put it toward first-year living
expenses. Put extra cash toward student loans. Have more money to
save and give away.

Amy and I are approaching fifteen years of marriage. Our wedding was nice but on the cheaper side. She still has regrets over our
choice in photographers and wedding cake. Our discontentment
with our own wedding cake grew after watching shows like *Ace of
Cakes, Cake Boss,* and *Food Network Challenge.* Now that we have a
few more bucks, I plan on nice anniversary parties and vow renewals
in the future. We'll do what we can afford now that we've been married longer, and we'll still be able to give to our church and missions
generously. What you cannot afford to do in your wedding now, wait
for later when you have more money.

Fox Alert: Wedding Planners

Don't allow the planning of a megawedding delay the bud of your love. And don't allow someone to force his or her dream wedding on you, even if that someone is your mom.

The Cohabitation Delay

It is unnecessary and unbiblical for you to live together before you get married. Researchers say that as many as 60 percent of young people today will cohabitate before marrying. The most common reason given is to "give it a trial run," an attitude stemming from the concern of ending up with a marriage like their parents.

Cohabitation is essentially when couples resort to a "trial marriage" to test commitment without permanence. It leaves them a "back door" while they try to enjoy the benefits of combined expenses, convenient sex, companionship, and freedom.

In 1960 there were 439,000 cohabitating couples in the United States alone. In 2006 that number jumped to 5,368,000. Mike and Harriett McManus pointed out that millions of cohabitating couples never marry: "Contrary to what they may think, couples who decide to live together are not postponing making a decision about marriage but are actually making a decision *not* to marry. Cohabitating is not a way to prepare for marriage but a way to prolong singleness."[4]

Steve and Jen enjoyed a "trial marriage" while they waited for the real thing. They started attending our church back in 2004. They fell in love with our church, but more importantly they fell in love with Jesus. They gave their hearts to Christ shortly after visiting Woodland Hills.

When they asked me to marry them, I put the date on my calendar but told them they would need extensive premarital counseling before I let them say "I do." Amy and I planned to meet with them for their first session over dinner at the Olive Garden. On the way to dinner I told Amy that I would confront them on the fact that they were living together. I wanted to confront this early in the meal so we would have time to process and Steve could throw things at me if he felt that was necessary.

"You sure know how to ruin a good meal," Amy said.

"I know, but Steve and Jen will handle this well," I replied.

I was half right. Jen agreed immediately. Steve needed some time. They both wanted to do the right thing, but Steve needed to crunch the numbers and understand the request. Steve asked if moving into a different room of the house would work but retracted his request when my eyes peered over the top of my glasses.

Several days after that dinner, Steve called me to say that he had moved into a friend's house. Hallelujah! After that, Steve and Jen were baptized together, completed premarital counseling, and were married. They had an outdoor wedding, surrounded by their family, friends, and small group. They now live in Gilbert, Arizona, and remain our dear friends to this day.

The eHarmony Delay (aka The Soul Mate Delay)

The right one might be right in front of you. Perhaps your unnecessary delay is the direct result of your whacked-out beliefs about compatibility. I am a fan of online dating and have performed many ceremonies for couples who met on a matchmaking site. However, be careful while using an online site that you do not fall for some of the promises or false teachings, such as the "soul mate" myth.

Sitting at home waiting for a "match" or for your phone to ring is like expecting a call from a company that never received your resume. Your "soul mate" is not floating around on this earth waiting for the right moment to bump into you. Gary Thomas wrote,

> There's a prevailing passivity among many young people who mistakenly think that God will "bring the right person along when the time is right."
>
> After high school, did you wait at home without applying to a single college, "trusting God" to motivate a university to write to you with an offer of admission because "God led them to"?
>
> Of course not!
>
> After college, do you plan to wait at home, "trusting God" that a company will "find you" after hearing about your sterling academic career?
>
> I hope not—or else, welcome to welfare.[5]

Online matchmaking grew in popularity shortly after Amy and I married. We often kid each other about how we might have been scored on those compatibility tests. Would the online sites have matched us up?

Young couples struggling in a bad marriage will ask the question, "Did I marry the wrong person?" In couples' counseling they might say things such as, "That's easy for you, Ted; you have a great marriage."

I'm thrilled to say that I have a great marriage, but it didn't just happen. Our first seven years, like most young marriages, were extremely tough. We fought regularly, endured long periods of the silent treatment, and had plenty of unmet expectations—but we worked through it. We kept the commitment we made on our wedding day and pushed through the pain and struggles.

On several occasions, young husbands or wives have tried to convince me that the person with whom they are having an affair is the one God wants them with. Silliness and stupidity is all that is! They try feeding me a slightly altered version of the "grass is greener" speech. I always remind them, "Where the grass is greener, there is a septic tank leaking." Don't step in that patch of grass!

I have no problem at all with you meeting someone online. Half the weddings I conduct are for young people who met online. So long as you go through the proper marriage preparation and both of you love and serve Jesus, I say, let's have a wedding.

Fox Alert: Compatibility Tests

I've always been a horrible test taker, and I don't believe a test can guarantee someone's ability to remain faithful for life. If you meet someone through an online dating service, you will still need a serious season of face-to-face time.

The Independence Delay

Many blogs and self-help articles advocating delayed marriage share a common thread. Some believe that a person must experience independence prior to marriage in order to be successful as a husband or wife.

Here's one example: "Confidence [developed before marriage] helps you to be a better partner and be more secure in a marriage relationship. People who are insecure can feel desperate to cling onto their partners and yet may have difficulty making compromises because they fear losing themselves if they do. Feeling confident in your identity makes being flexible easier and less threatening."[6]

Independence trumps oneness in a marriage. As a pastor who regularly does marriage counseling, I see independence as one of the leading causes of marital conflict. At the root of couples in crisis you'll often find two people trying to live independent lives. They no longer dream together. They don't attend church together anymore. They forget to pray together. Perhaps they have different spending patterns and parenting styles. She begins looking for intimacy from other sources. And he turns to attention from other women or masturbation rather than intimacy with his wife. Satan fed the independence line to Eve when he said, "For God knows that when you eat of it your eyes will be opened, and you will be like God, knowing good and evil" (Gen. 3:5). If we're not careful, we can start to believe the lie and try to live independent of God and others.

When Genesis 2:24 says "united to his wife," the word *united* means "to cling, stay close, cleave, stick to, stick with, follow closely, and join to." The goal of marriage is to weave your own dreams, goals, and passions into the dreams, goals, and passions of your spouse. That's part of oneness.

Delayed-marriage advocates say you should get married only after you've been successful living independently. A better way to solve the independence delay is to take 100 percent personal responsibility for your sin, feelings, thoughts, and actions and be joined to your spouse, who is 100 percent responsible for his or her sin, feelings, thoughts, and actions. Personal responsibility can help create a great marriage; independence does not.

The Age Delay

Determining the right age to marry can be difficult. Divorce has many causes beyond age. When you research the factors contributing to divorce, you find that age, religion, occupation, region of the country, race, poverty, cohabitation, whether or not you had alcoholic parents, smoking, and current events all affect divorce rates.[7]

So in the midst of all this, yes, determining the right age for marriage is a major challenge. You'll get a different answer depending on whom you ask. In my casual, independent research I've discovered that most people won't answer with an exact age. Restrictions regarding age can be confusing even for kids. My children get frustrated with the inconsistencies of seat-belt laws, kids' menus, rules, height restrictions, and school milestones.

For example, over the past few months, I've been studying the children's menus at every restaurant we frequent. Strangely, the age of adulthood differs depending on the restaurant we're in. At our favorite pizza buffet, both of my children get kids' prices. But in five years, according to the pizza place, my seven-year-old will be an adult. Corynn will also be considered an adult at Silver Dollar City, our local theme park. Although at Disney World, she apparently matures faster and becomes an adult at ten years old.

In his book *Men of Honor, Women of Virtue,* my friend Chuck Stecker shared more of this age confusion:

One time I was speaking in Idaho but staying in a hotel across the state line in Oregon. The laws in the two states concerning adulthood were actually different for just such things as the use of pools and hot tubs. In one state you were considered adult enough to be in the hot tub by yourself at age thirteen; but if you crossed the state line, you had to be fifteen. Think about this for a moment: You could actually step across the state line and lose your adulthood for more than two years. Easy come, easy go.[8]

Let's look at some common milestones for kids and adults:

Age 3	Start paying full fare for flights
Age 5	Start kindergarten
Age 10	Become an adult at Disney
Age 12	Become an adult at major chain restaurants
Age 15	Learner's permit for drivers in Florida and Texas
Age 15½	Learner's permit for drivers in California and Virginia
Age 16	Learner's permit for drivers in Maryland and Pennsylvania
Age 16	Begin dating (most common age for parents' permission)
Age 18	Vote and smoke
Age 21	Drink alcohol
Age 25	Rent a car

As you can see, we get mixed messages about age and adulthood. I love explaining these things to my son: "No, on this ride you need to be four years old. Now on this ride you need to be forty-two inches tall. Sorry, the slide is for two-year-olds and younger."

As you might expect, the "right" age for marriage can be just as confusing.

Most of our parents and grandparents got jobs when they were teens. Some of them even dropped out of school to work full-time in order to provide for their families. Their parents doled out responsibility in large quantities and earlier in life. For us, it's a different story. I believe that the age delay has its roots in the Buster generation.

My grandparents were part of the Builder generation. Born between 1922 and 1943, they lived through both the Great Depression and World War II. They valued hard work and respect for authority, and most of them married young. Their generation was built on survival and sacrifice. Some dropped out of high school to join the military and fought to save the world for us. They got married as teenagers and were forced to grow up. They were not afforded the luxury of a prolonged stage of adolescence. Marrying young was simply expected because their parents believed that marriage should happen at the beginning of adulthood.

My parents were part of the Boomer generation. Born between 1943 and 1960, their defining experiences included the mainstream use of television, the civil rights movement, and prosperity. Their values did not mirror their parents' values. Survival was not their chief goal. This generation values health and wellness, personal growth, and success.

The Busters, born between 1960 and 1980, were the first generation in which delayed marriage became common. This generation values diversity, global thinking, and independence, and they are marrying later and later.

This delay is the primary reason I wrote *Young and in Love*. I wanted to help the young people in our congregation who heard, "You're too young to get married." I wanted to give them answers and practical help. You may not agree with every argument in this book, and that's okay. But I want to give you a better answer than those who tell you, "Wait until you are older."

Check out www.youngandinlove.com for video podcasts, articles, and resources to help you prepare for marriage.

Young and in Love Marriage Journal

What are some ways you can financially prepare for marriage without delaying?

Outline a reasonable budget for a wedding ceremony that avoids debt but still gives you a great start to your married life.

What is your plan for jobs, education, and marriage?

Would you say your maturity level is ahead of or behind others your age?

Fox Alert: Bad Counseling

A title behind a name does not a great counselor make. Your marriage counselor may have a business card that reads "LMFT" (Licensed Marriage and Family Therapist), but that does not guarantee that her or she will give you good advice. Make sure you get biblical counseling and not arbitrary, cultural advice packaged as counseling. Beware! There are many therapists who, in my opinion, give out horrible advice and dishonor the institution of marriage.

Chapter 7

Age, Privilege, and Responsibility

Don't let anyone look down on you because you
are young, but set an example for the believers in
speech, in life, in love, in faith and in purity.

—1 Timothy 4:12

Marriage is our last, best chance to grow up.

—Joseph Barth

When I first started in ministry I was shocked by how much the older
people of the church struggled with the immaturity of the younger people.

At my first church, I was the twenty-two-year-old associate pastor, and I served with a twenty-six-year-old senior pastor. We attended
countless deacons' meetings where we were told, "You guys need to settle
down. One day you'll be like us, and you'll understand things better.
You're young and will eventually calm down."

I've also had the opportunity to transition two churches from traditional to contemporary worship style. Both were Baptist churches, one in Texas and another in Georgia. The pastors hired me specifically to make the transition in worship styles. They both basically told me, "We are officially calling you the sacrificial lamb because I hope they slaughter you and not me." It was a struggle to watch the older members of these churches as they chose their traditions and preferences over the tastes of their children and grandchildren.

I've waited my whole life to be old. Most people dread age forty, but I welcome it. Last year Amy noticed my first strands of gray hair, and I was thrilled. She thinks I need help. But my entire life has been spent hanging out with people older than me. At church, on family holidays, and at school, I could always be found hanging around the old people. I found their conversations more stimulating and their activities more challenging. To this day, my two best friends in the ministry are seventy and sixty-three years old.

First Timothy is a New Testament book written by an older pastor instructing a younger pastor. The church in Ephesus was dealing with leadership issues, and in this letter Paul warned young Timothy to not give up in the midst of older leaders who "despise[d]" his youth (4:12 ESV). The term *youth* in Timothy's day was used for those under the age of forty. Timothy was probably in his early thirties.

Paul told Timothy to "labor and strive" (v. 10) "so that everyone may see your progress" (v. 15). We see in this letter that age and wisdom are not synonymous. You may be waiting to grow old so that you can be wise. Wisdom often comes with old age, but I've met plenty of seniors lacking wisdom. What I found to be true of many of those older people who tried to stifle younger people in the church was this: At some point in their lives they made the decision to stop growing and to stop learning. They made a conscious decision to stop making progress in their faith, work, and marriage.

However, Paul told Timothy to stay in his position of authority and not to "let anyone look down on you because you are young" (v. 12). *Young* is a relative term. My father-in-law, Denny, is sixty-two years old and a greeter at Walmart here in Branson. He is called "Sonny" at least once a day. He is much younger than most of the people who borrow those electric carts at the front door of the store, but at the same time, some of those customers are the meanest people on planet Earth. They even have foul mouths. They stopped making progress years ago.

Paul suggested three different responses to someone who despises your youth. These suggestions will serve you well if you receive criticism for your decision to marry young. First, "set an example for the believers in speech, in life, in love, in faith and in purity" (v. 12); second, make progress in your life and doctrine (v. 16); and finally, "do not rebuke an older man harshly" but treat him like a father (5:1). Here we see the theme of honor again.

When older people say you are "too young," prove them wrong with your mouth, behavior, faith, purity, and doctrine and by the way you honor them despite their attitude.

Fox Alert: Grumpy Old People

Ecclesiastes 12:1 says, "Remember your Creator in the days of your youth, before the days of trouble come and the years approach when you will say, 'I find no pleasure in them.'" Growing old is hard, and everybody responds in different ways to the process. I have several senior men and women in my life who are a pure joy to be around. They love Jesus and those around them, and they've responded well to the trials of life. But others in their senior years have allowed the pain and struggles of life to affect their attitudes in a negative way rather than a biblical way, as outlined in James 1:2–4 and Romans 5:3–5. Never listen to the advice of one who says something bitter or negative like, "You'll settle down," or "We were in love like that once; you'll get over it." Do not allow the negativity someone else has allowed into his or her life to become part of yours. Enjoy life and marriage. Find loving, kind older friends and model your marriage after theirs.

Choose Your Statistic

I hate statistics. Not just because they are boring but also because they are limiting. When you read a statistic like "50 percent of marriages will end in divorce," you might think about placing your marriage in the 50 percent of couples who divorce rather than the 50 percent who stay together. Some of us tend to see the glass half-empty. Research has its limitations, so be careful not to become a statistical pessimist.

For example, our country is currently experiencing the worst recession of my lifetime. Our unemployment rate is almost at 10 percent (never mind the fact that Haiti's unemployment rate is 84 percent). *Nevertheless, we whine.*

As a pastor, I see unemployed members in our church family. What we forget about is the fact that 90 percent of America is still working. I am not in a position to change the national unemployment rate. But I can try to change the situation of the next unemployed dad who walks through my door. Perhaps I can be his pastor and help him move into the 90 percent who are working.

The same thing is true with couples. Gary Smalley, my mentor and founder of the Smalley Relationship Center, has operated for years under the following mission statement: "Reduce the divorce rate; increase marital satisfaction." Gary is a visionary. Maybe I'm a lesser leader, but I have chosen a different mission: "Do for one marriage what you can't do for all."

If I woke up every morning with the humongous vision of decreasing the divorce rate in America, I would be setting myself up for mental failure. But if I go to work with the plan to keep one couple from divorcing, then not only am I fulfilling the Great Commission, but I'm also working to move couples to the good side of the statistical equation. Whether it's writing a book, preparing for a conference or sermon, or counseling a couple, I get to help one marriage at a time.

The same is true for you. Age and wisdom are not synonymous. I know believers of all ages who lack in wisdom, judgment, and commitment. One of my struggles with the research encouraging you to wait until age twenty-five or thirty for marriage is that it does not take into account the level of wisdom or maturity of the individual. It clumps you into national averages mixed with believers, agnostics, and non-Christians. So once again, I say be careful of statistics—they do not have to apply to you.

You can do nothing about your age or what the statistics say. You can do everything about your own personal maturity level. When you're told, "You're too young," try to discern if what the person is really saying is, "You are still an adolescent," or "You have some more growing up to do." Sometimes blaming your age is a more polite and socially acceptable way of saying, "It's time to grow up!"

Too Much Privilege, Not Enough Responsibility

My daughter, Corynn, is convinced that she's never leaving home. At seven, she's made up her mind that Mom and Dad take such good care of her that she'll just stay.

But she knows I'll have none of that.

One of the hardest questions Corynn has ever asked me is, "Dad, who do you love more, me or Mom?"

Ouch! Naturally, my first response to a question like that is to act like I didn't hear the question or to squint my eyes as though I didn't understand the question. She has me wrapped around her little finger.

"I love your mommy and you both," I say gently, "but God wants me to love Mommy in a different way. Your mommy and I are together for life. We will be together until one of us goes to heaven or Jesus returns. But you, Corynn, will not be with us forever. You will one day leave our home and start a family of your own."

Corynn is quick to reply, "I want to be with you and Mommy forever."

"You can't be with us forever, Corynn," I say.

As tears form in her eyes, she glares at me and says, "I am going to college online and staying home forever. You can't make me leave." While I must admit I like the sound of that from a tuition stand-point, I need her to know that separation from Mom and Dad is actually a sign of health and maturity. She will need to leave home one day.

Of course, part of me wants her to stay home. But I've been handed the assignment of starting Corynn on her spiritual journey for life. I won't be with her for three quarters of her life, but God gave me this time on the front end to invest in her and to help form the beliefs of her heart.

There's a very important verse in the Bible that speaks to parenting and the subject of prolonged adolescence. The famous "leave and cleave" texts of the Bible are most often taught to adults: "For this reason a man will leave his father and mother and be united to his wife, and they will become one flesh" (Gen. 2:24). Jesus repeated this verse in Matthew, and Paul repeated it in Ephesians. The King James Version uses the word *cleave* to convey being united. These words, first given in the garden of Eden, were given to a couple with no biological parents. One must wonder if God was instructing Adam and Eve on how they were to raise their children, rather than giving them a teaching for their own marriage. If this was true, then this teaching would be given to children, not adults. We have no record of the talk, but I wonder when Adam and Eve first taught Genesis 2:24 to Cain and Abel and later Seth? I'm thinking earlier, rather than later.

Marriage involves a new priority. When you see the word *leave* you may think you need to move a thousand miles away from your mom and dad. However, the focus of this text is not *geographical*. Most young couples actually live in close proximity to their parents and move away later. The focus of this text is *relational*.

"Leaving" is the idea that no relationship, apart from your relationship with God, is more important than your marriage. To leave means to forsake, depart from, leave behind, and abandon. And I believe that leaving home at a relatively young age is the primary antidote to the problem of prolonged adolescence.

We parents today teach our kids how to be dependent on us rather than how to live independent of us. The term *adolescence* stems from the Latin *adolescere*, which means "to grow up." This man-made age is a period of time when a person is no longer a child but not yet an adult. I call it limbo. Others call adolescence a vacation from responsibility.

From the time God spoke Genesis 2:24 and through the first several thousand years of human history, kids grew up and became adults. There was no intermediate state of being. It's only been in the past one hundred years or so that kids delay growing up and we've inserted this ten-to-fifteen-year stretch between childhood and adulthood. I find it funny, however, how the Bible uses only the terms *child* and *adult*. Biblically, there is no gap between the two. Children simply become adults. While Scripture gives many responsibilities to parents, the apostle Paul summed it up this way: "Fathers, do not exasperate your children; instead, bring them up in the training and instruction of the Lord" (Eph. 6:4). Our job as parents is to instruct our children and keep their hearts open so that when they become adults they have a love for the Lord that pleases God.

However, we've prolonged adolescence to the point that researchers have coined a new term for the gap between adolescence and adulthood. Come on, seriously? I'm sorry, but I'm pounding on the computer right now as I insert the following text:

Researchers, sociologists and psychologists say there's a new phase of life—only recently acknowledged—that covers this gap between adolescence and adulthood. What was once the purview of academia has crossed into the popular culture. A plethora of how-to-cope books are declaring a worldwide shift in what it means to be an adult.

"It's the harbinger of a basic transformation of adulthood," says James Côté, a sociologist at the University of Western Ontario who has coined the term "youthhood." "The traditional adulthood of duty and self-sacrifice is becoming more and more a thing of the past."[1]

If you're not worn out or upset by what you just read, welcome to *youthhood*. It's bad enough that we've created a gap between childhood and adulthood, adolescence—now we have to create a term for the growing gap between adolescence and adulthood. Yikes!

As a lead pastor, I have hired many college graduates to serve at our church, and many of these young people have frustrated me considerably. I used to think that twentysomethings were lazy and disrespectful of authority. But I've come to learn that many times I'm the first person in their lives to challenge them out of adolescence and into adulthood. As their first full-time employer, many times I have to do what their parents should have done.

Becoming an adult means leaving home, making wise adult decisions, and taking responsibility for the outcome of those decisions.

Most parents today try to control their teen's behavior rather than monitor the behavior. In my opinion, parents wait too long to teach their kids to be adults, and as a result, intentionally or unintentionally, they're prolonging their journey into adulthood.

But don't stress out. If you grew up in a home where your mom and dad handed you privilege and withheld responsibility, there's still something you can do about it. You can choose to value responsibility above privilege. You can begin to see privilege as something you gain after a long season of responsibility.

Did the Boomers spoil their kids? Yes. Is there something wrong with being handed privilege? No. The key is to link the two. Kids need our practical and emotional support, but when should parents start giving that practical support? When should kids be taught how to write a check, do their taxes, clock in at work, and give to their church? I'll tell you this much—I've yet to meet a parent who says, "I do not want to raise responsible adults." What nobody knows is when to start preparing them. We start with privilege at a very early age and delay responsibility. I believe that this responsibility delay is one reason we are now delaying marriage across an entire generation.

I want my children to learn maturity at an early age. Amy and I define maturity in our home as "knowing I will not be with Mom and Dad forever and planning accordingly." We believe that separation from parents is good and healthy. Good parenting recognizes the blessing that children need to one day be released into a new journey with Christ and their mate. They need to be encouraged and full of confidence that they will one day make capable, adult decisions on their own. I don't want my kids waiting until age twenty-five or thirty to gain that confidence.

I talk to adult children all the time who are still calling home in their twenties and thirties asking their parents for money. Then they get frustrated with their "controlling" parents. My first counsel to them is to get the Star Wars bedsheets off the bed. It's time to grow up!

When I do premarital counseling, I make sure young couples get this. The conversation usually goes something like this: "Before you call home, asking for money, think through the interest payments. You have no idea how much it will cost you to borrow two hundred dollars to meet your rent payment. You will pay on that loan for years. You will pay the interest through lack of trust, controlling maneuvers, and occasional guilt trips." It would be cheaper and easier to get a second job to cover your rent than to ask your parents.

Proverbs 23:22–25 says, "Listen to your father, who gave you life, and do not despise your mother when she is old. Buy the truth and do not sell it; get wisdom, discipline and understanding. The father of a righteous man has great joy; he who has a wise son delights in him. May your father and mother be glad." As a parent, I want to delight in my children, and I want to know that our journey in Christ has rubbed off on their lives. I want to look at Carson and Corynn and say, "You are my son and daughter, and I am well pleased."

In researching for this book, I read many books trying to get into the minds of twentysomethings. Each book I read shared ways for the church to better minister to this age group. In some cases the author asked the church to be an extension of the home and help prolong adolescence. I won't do it. I love the twentysomethings in my church too much to give them too much privilege while withholding responsibility.

"They're not as mature because they're not required to be," said Jeffrey Jensen Arnett, a developmental psychologist, talking about twentysomethings. "It's really the society and culture as a whole."

"This is a generation that has grown up in an accelerated culture and forced them to be older before they're ready," David Morrison, president of Twentysomething Inc., said. "Now that they have their independence, they are going to squeeze every ounce of that sponge before they settle down."[2]

Dad and Me

My dad did not believe in prolonged adolescence. Come to find out, he didn't even believe in adolescence. His plan for his kids was simple: childhood to adulthood and no vacation in between. He simply placed greater value on responsibility than privilege, and as a result, I've been working my whole life.

I remember driving home one night with my dad when he noticed a neighbor's yard running amok. He stopped the car and challenged me to approach the neighbor with my services. So I did. For ten bucks, I said, I'd mow this man's "field." To an eight-year-old, when the grass grows higher than eighteen inches, it no longer constitutes a lawn. The man smiled and jumped at my offer. It took me two days to give him back his yard. Was my dad done? Nope. He had more to teach me, and lesson two was about money management. At his desk in the basement we split the money by giving $1.00 tithe to the church, $.50 to missions, $5.00 to savings, and $3.50 to spend. Almost thirty years later, I still tithe, give to missions, and save. Funny how that works.

Roy Chestnut, my childhood pastor, also taught me about responsibility. As I was approaching the dreaded junior-high years, our church started a building project that would more than double the size of our facility. My pastor could have easily rented a machine to cut the ten ditches needed for the drain pipes, but he decided to hire the junior-high boys instead. This decision would probably cost him more time, money, and angst, but he saw a bigger kingdom investment. The ditches needed to be thirty-six inches deep and run for hundreds of yards—and would be dug by twelve-year-olds with a spade. He paid us five dollars an hour. I was good at math and very happy!

On my thirteenth birthday, January 29, 1987, I got a very special surprise. It was a card from the IRS with a 1099. I was thrilled to report to my parents that I had made over $7,500 in 1986 at the age of twelve. Dad was proud. I could see it in his eyes. But I could also see another lesson coming. He had already taught me how to tithe, give, and save—now it was time to meet Uncle Sam.

Believe it or not, the biggest fight my dad and I ever got into was over my taxes that year. My dad volunteered to do my taxes. Since my work at the church was considered contract labor, I was self-employed. I was responsible for both halves of the Social Security tax, which was over 15 percent at the time. I immediately became a fan of country music and the Ray Stevens song "If Ten Percent Is Good Enough for Jesus (It Oughta Be Enough for Uncle Sam)."

Dad found out that my tax burden was almost $1,000. My dad broke the news gently to me by saying, "Ted, I'm writing a check out of your savings account for this amount." I went right at him and said, "Dad, no way. We're not paying that. They don't expect twelve-year-olds to pay Social Security." I vividly remember being in attack mode. I wonder how many parents today are getting into arguments with their tweens over taxes?

He later overheard me on the phone with tax attorneys and accountants trying to verify the rule that twelve-year-olds had to pay taxes. He got angrier than I had ever seen him before or since, and there were many days of slamming doors and phones in our home. We both got angry and for different reasons. But in the end, my dad was right. Go figure!

I love my dad and praise my Father in heaven for a man named Ron Cunningham. He was man enough to teach his boys responsibility at an early age. My family is thankful as well!

Check out www.youngandinlove.com for video podcasts, articles, and resources to help you prepare for marriage.

Young and in Love Marriage Journal

What word best describes the home you grew up in? Privilege or responsibility?

What are you doing now to grow in personal responsibility?

Name a few of the older foxes trying to deter your young love. Now think about several ways you can show them honor.

Fox Alert: Statistics

Don't let statistics scare or deter you from young love. I have a great marriage in a country with a 50 percent divorce rate. I made the decision to be a part of the statistic who stays married, to choose that statistic for us. If both you and your spouse will commit to that, then you, too, can be in the 50 percent who stay married.

Chapter 8

Character

Be imitators of God, therefore, as dearly loved children.

—Ephesians 5:1

Moral laxity is the number one cause of divorce in this country. Debt, adultery, and broken promises are symptoms of a spouse's lack of character. Shallow integrity leads couples to look for an easy out when they find themselves on the poorer side of "for richer or poorer" or on the sick side of "in sickness and in health."

Tom, the Hebrew word for integrity, means "to be complete or solid." Psalm 78:72 uses *tom* to speak of the integrity of the heart: "So he shepherded them according to the integrity *[tom]* of his heart, and guided them with his skillful hands" (NASB).

I love Pastor Chuck Swindoll's practical application of the Scriptures. He does a fantastic job of describing what integrity is and what it is not:

> Integrity is completeness or soundness…. You have
> integrity if you keep your promises…. If you are a
> person of integrity, you will do what you say. What
> you declare, you will do your best to be….
>
> But there are some things integrity is not. It is
> not sinless perfection. A person with integrity does
> not live a life absolutely free of sin. No one does.
> But one with integrity quickly acknowledges his
> failures and doesn't hide the wrong.[1]

Marriages fall apart because of deep character issues, not because of surface issues. You may like the way a person looks and behaves in public, but if he or she has no character or integrity, then you're in trouble. Character is everything.

Inspect Your Shade Tree

In 2007, my wife and I built a house. We own a heavily wooded lot outside of town and made the decision to be our own general contractors. We hired the excavators, framers, plumbers, electricians, and over twenty other subcontractors to complete the house. Who were we trying to fool? Watching HGTV several times a week does not make you a building contractor. But you have to give us props for trying. Our marriage survived too.

"Where do we put the house?" was our first question. The three-acre lot was mixed with cedars and oaks, and smack-dab in the middle of the lot was a one-hundred-year-old oak tree. This thing was huge and could provide shade for the whole house. So we positioned the house with this tree in the backyard, so it would provide shade from the intense afternoon sun. After clearing a half acre, we stood back to look at this majestic, perfectly shaped oak tree. We had seen an oak tree just like this before in corporate logos such as the one used by Cancer Treatment Centers of America. B-E-A-*utiful!*

One problem though: We didn't inspect the tree well enough before making the decision to clear the land around it. The tree is completely hollow. Oops! Things are not always as they appear. This decaying tree is resting fifteen feet from the house, and even now it leans toward our master bedroom.

Solomon was a shade tree for his Shullamite fiancée: "Like an apple tree among the trees of the forest is my lover among the young men. I delight to sit in his shade, and his fruit is sweet to my taste" (Song 2:3). Before you choose a shade tree, make sure he or she is not hollow on the inside. Inspect the tree *and* the fruit to ensure that you will have shade in your relationship for the next fifty years.

I may get another year or two out of the oak still standing in our backyard, but I'll need to take it down before it falls.

The Four Cs

Character is the first of four Cs needed to inspect the shade of the person you are dating or engaged to. For me, this is the only non-negotiable of the Cs. The other three Cs—chemistry, competency, and calling—are not deal breakers for me. He or she can be a doctor, lawyer, pastor, or plumber, but if the person you marry has no character, then you'll have problems in your marriage. He or she can have a strong personality or be fun loving, but if there's no integrity, then chemistry doesn't matter.

Your character determines your commitment in marriage. Since the average length of first marriages in the United States today is eight years,[2] commitment is the essential ingredient that will help you build a lifetime of enjoying each other. The reason commitment is not a fifth C is because character and commitment are synonymous. If the one you marry has no character, do not walk down the aisle.

The prophet Malachi linked character to commitment when he said, "The LORD is acting as the witness between you and the wife of your youth, because you have broken faith with her, though she is your partner, the wife of your marriage covenant" (2:14). Due to a lack of character, many young couples hire a pastor only to serve as a justice of the peace rather than holding a ceremony where the Lord serves as both witness and judge of character. Many years ago, young couples would go to the church and submit themselves to the spiritual authority there to receive a blessing to marry.

Nowadays, young people come to the church to have the leaders validate their spouse selection. Usually, they want a church wedding but not necessarily a spiritual marriage. At Woodland Hills, when one of the pastors begins to explain what a church wedding entails, many couples seek out a pastor from another church. Our initial guidelines are simple. You can't be having sex prior to marriage. You can't live together before your wedding. You must be committed to each other for life. We don't have a lot of guidelines, but we do ask, "How much do you want the church and the community at Woodland Hills Family Church to be involved in holding you accountable?"

My premarital counseling always begins with this first C. I begin by asking each person about his or her personal faith journey. Here are some of the answers I have received:

"I've always been a Christian."

"I was baptized as a baby."

"I come from a religious family."

"My parents have taken me to church since I was born."

"I've always believed in God."

"I attend Woodland Hills."

None of these answers work for me. A decision to follow Jesus at Vacation Bible School at age eight, or a walk to the altar at summer camp at age thirteen is not enough of an answer. And if it's not enough for the leader of the church, it should not be enough for you either. You need to ask more probing questions of your potential spouse.

Here's a better list of questions to start probing his or her character:

Is he or she an active follower of Jesus (not just a church attendee)?

Does he or she honor and respect others? Parents?

How does he or she handle money?

Is he or she angry or hot tempered?

Does he or she follow through on commitments?

Does he or she demonstrate respect for authority?

Is he or she entitled?

Most of these questions can be answered by simply watching behavior. Everything we do as believers should point to Jesus. Your responsibility and mine is to make sure everything about our lives points to Jesus. Integrity can be easily identified at restaurants, malls, school, and parents' homes.

Once you've established that the one you love is deeply committed to Jesus, you need to go a little further. There are some character qualities unique to the genders because men and women have different struggles and temptations.

His Character
Is He a One-Woman Man?

Dallas Seminary professor Howard Hendricks is known for saying, "Every man struggles with lust. If not, he's got another problem." Men must learn to control their flesh. The apostle Paul listed the "one-woman man" characteristic in the list of qualifications for leaders in the church (1 Tim. 3:12). Single guys remain a one-woman man by not fantasizing about sleeping with another man's wife. In other words, they can't download porn and cheat on their future wife.

In ministry, I've been made fun of a lot by pastor friends and leaders for being somewhat aloof. I admit that I am not touchy-feely, and honestly, Amy's opinion is the only one that matters. She tells me regularly, "Ted, don't let people get down on you too much for being aloof, because I enjoy that. I am thrilled to know that you will never meet with a woman alone or eat out with a woman from the church. You put practices and steps into your life to make sure you are a one-woman man."

Guys, we have to guard ourselves in this area. I perform a lot of weddings each year, and it kills me to think that the father walking his princess down the aisle may be handing her over to a sex addict of some kind. Daddy has cared for her heart for twenty years, and now an unguarded, reckless boy is about to take her as his wife. His head is flooded with images with which she cannot compete. That is the reason that the first question I ask in premarital counseling is about his character.

Is He a Hard Worker?

Will he be able to provide for you and your family? Being a hard worker is different from what kind of work he will do. We will cover that in the competency C. I can promise you this: Twenty years into marriage, laziness is not cute. It will frustrate you beyond belief when you're trying to put your kids in braces and your husband's sitting around waiting for the "right opportunity."

Look for the guy who will work any job while waiting for the right job. We live in Branson, a town with over one hundred different music and variety shows. Countless artists move here each year hoping to land the perfect gig. I recently worked with a family in which the husband had been out of work for a year and a half, waiting to land a show that needed a brass player. His wife worked feverishly while the bank planned to take their home. It made me furious. Paul said this kind of guy "has denied the faith and is worse than an unbeliever" (1 Tim. 5:8). Such a man is unfaithful. Men work hard to earn money to spend on women and children, and that's good theology.

You want a guy who is a producer first, a consumer second. Pastor Mark Driscoll has a healthy disdain for a culture of boys who refuse to produce:

> The marketing sweet spot for many companies is young men ages eighteen to thirty-four. These

guys don't know what it means to be a man, and
so marketers fill the void with products that define
manhood by what you consume rather than what
you produce. The tough retrosexual guys consume women, porn, alcohol, drugs, television,
music, video games, toys, cars, sports, and fantasy
leagues.... The artsy, techie metrosexual types consume clothes, decaf lattes, shoes, gadgets, cars (not
trucks), furniture, hair products, and underwear
with the names of very important people on the
waistband.... Men are supposed to be producers,
not just consumers.[3]

For fifty dollars a month I keep a one-million-dollar life-
insurance policy, and it's my favorite bill each month. Dale Sanders
is my insurance man, and he has promised me that if something happens to me he will have a seven-figure check in Amy's hands within a
week. I love that. Taking care of my family is the top priority for me.
I do not want Amy or my children to struggle, and I will work hard
to make that happen.

Does He Submit Well to Authority?

You want to know that he will submit to the authority of
the church, older men, and his boss at work. Why? You should
marry a guy who can stand up to rebuke, correction, and sound
teaching. In our consumer culture, most people choose churches
based on music style, the coolness factor of the pastor, and stellar
children's ministries. They will stay at the church so long as their

needs are being met and no one rocks their boat. But how will your potential husband react when confronted with sin in his life? You may hit a spot in your marriage when counseling is necessary. At the very least, you may need the help of a church small group. If you get to this place, will your husband be the type of guy who hears only what he wants to hear? Will he have the guts to stick it out when chinks in his armor are revealed? You want a guy with a submissive attitude toward authority and a healthy disdain for entitlement.

Is He Easily Angered?

First Timothy 2:8 says this: "I want men everywhere to lift up holy hands in prayer, without anger or disputing." A man's character is quickly revealed in the way he deals with anger. In and of itself, anger is not a sin. It's a secondary emotion that typically stems from a primary emotion such as failure, rejection, or the feeling of being judged, controlled, or cheated. The issue is not so much what he gets angry about but rather what he does with his anger. Does he know how to resolve anger? How short is his fuse? How long does it take him to calm down? Does he always seem to be mad at someone or something? Does he take his anger out on you?

You never bury anger dead. Anger will always resurface in another relationship. Men tend to bring their anger from work home to their family. Those closest to them usually get the harshest treatment. And I often say that unresolved anger is like drinking poison, expecting the other person to get sick. Marry the guy who gets angry and then resolves his anger by seeking forgiveness and peace with himself and others. You do not want a toxic marriage.

Will He Be a Great Dad?

Ask yourself these questions: Will he be the type of guy who provokes his children to wrath? (Eph. 6:4). Will he be willing to spend a lot of time with the children (Deut. 6:7)? Will he be willing to give up hobbies and sports to spend time with his children?

Quality is no substitute for quantity when it comes to family time. In the ancient Hebrew culture, a child's education was the primary responsibility of the parents, not the responsibility of formal institutions or of government. Parents were responsible for teaching their children by modeling truth, by sharing God's Word in everyday conversation, and by experiencing life together. This was considered the best way to educate children: "And you must commit yourselves wholeheartedly to these commands that I am giving you today. Repeat them again and again to your children. Talk about them when you are at home and when you are on the road, when you are going to bed and when you are getting up" (Deut. 6:6–7 NLT).

Your husband-to-be should be a loving and firm dad who is not afraid to be the bad guy and discipline when necessary. He must set clearly defined limits in the home and enforce them firmly.

Is He Too Attached to His Mom, Hobbies, or Friends?

Does he understand the concept of boundaries? Will he call Mommy every time the two of you get into a fight? Many marriage problems in the early years stem from a guy who wants to continue to live the single life. Do his parents still buy him cars, phones, or clothes? When he is around his parents, are they clearly in control of his life? Benevolent parents can destroy marriages if you're not careful. Does he have the wherewithal to tell his mom and dad, "Hey, thank you for your generosity, but I don't need a new phone and I can buy my own dang clothes." Men, don't wait to have your parents set the boundaries, because some of them won't. You must take the lead and set the boundaries.

Also, is hanging with the boys on poker night still his highest priority? Does he say things like, "I need my downtime?" Oh brother! Be very sure that he is ready to grow up and let go of the Xbox and all-nighters with his friends before you marry him.

Fox Alert: Angry, Addicted, Lazy Men

Little boys make bad husbands. A boy who refuses to become a man is not ready to marry. A boy who refuses to get a job is not ready to marry. And a boy who masturbates to pornography is not a guy you want to marry. He comes with many issues that will keep your marriage from blooming.

Her Character

Spawned by an agenda of Satan, young women today are being fed lies such as don't get married, be your own woman, and don't have children. Some call it the feminist movement. If you stay single, you'll be liberated.

Marriage and celibacy, whichever you choose, are meant to bring glory to God, not to feed some self-centered idea. Guys, is the woman you plan to marry influenced by the world or by Christ? Before you provide shade to a woman for a lifetime, be sure her life reflects the gospel.

Is She a Busybody or Malicious Talker?

Idleness causes sin. Nothing brings embarrassment to a husband more than an out-of-control, gossipy wife. The apostle Paul told widows under the age of sixty to marry and have children because he was concerned their idleness would turn them into busybodies (1 Tim. 5:9–14). He didn't want them to become destructive to other homes. Scripture is very clear that out of the overflow of the heart the mouth speaks (Matt. 15:18). If you marry a woman who is constantly running down people with her mouth, be warned. That will one day turn on you: "A quarrelsome wife is as annoying as constant dripping on a rainy day. Stopping her complaints is like trying to stop the wind or trying to hold something with greased hands" (Prov. 27:15–16 NLT).

Is She Moody?

Marry a temperate woman. The opposite of temperate is moody. With a moody woman, you never know which woman you are getting. One of the things I love about my wife is that she is easy to get along with. Every woman has mood swings (just as men do), and we all have our ups and downs in life. I'm not speaking of menstrual cycles or even mental-health issues but rather the nastiness that can come from an unguarded woman.

When I pull in my driveway every night, do you know the thing I am most grateful for in Amy Cunningham? She is steady. I don't pull into the driveway at night thinking, *Father, which woman am I getting tonight?* I have friends who do feel that way. I have friends who pull into their driveways at night and think, *Father in heaven, I love You with all of my heart. Please give me the good wife tonight.*

I don't want the moody one. Even if Amy has had a long, hard, and frustrating day, she knows how to work through it. You know why? She has character, and she allows God to work in her. (Caution: Men can be just as moody as women and can easily neglect the feelings of their wives. Do not use the "moody test" as an excuse to *not* listen to your wife.)

Is She Modest?

Women get distracted from Jesus when they act immodestly. The apostle Paul cautioned women not to allow their dress to become a distraction to the gospel: "I also want women to dress modestly, with decency and propriety, not with braided hair or gold or pearls or expensive clothes, but with good deeds, appropriate for women who profess to worship God" (1 Tim. 2:9–10).

Ladies, save the crack for the drug dealers and the plumbers. Guys, if you're turned on by a woman who shows off her thong above her jeans as part of her normal wardrobe, think twice. Do you really want to be with someone who presents her body in a way that leads men to lust?

While we were on vacation this past summer, we stopped to eat at a Japanese steakhouse. At the grill across from us was a high school girls' graduation party, and the girls wore some questionable attire.

I looked at my six-year-old daughter and said, "Corynn, you know your dad loves you, right?"

She said, "Yeah, Daddy."

I said, "I want you to look over at those girls right there, and I want you to look very carefully at what they are wearing." I said,

"Corynn, you will never wear clothes like that, ever. Do you know why?"

"Why, Daddy?" she asked.

I said, "Because your daddy loves you." Then I continued, "Corynn, I'm sad because I think some of those girls have a daddy who doesn't love them very much. Corynn, I'm going to keep saying it and saying it so you'll always know it. Those girls got ripped off. The dress is supposed to be high on the top, low on the bottom. They bought a broken dress, Corynn. It's low on the top and high on the bottom; they should get their money back. I hope they didn't pay full price for that. Corynn, underwear isn't meant to be seen."

You might be asking, "Ted, are you against fancy underwear?" Absolutely not! I love them! They are wonderful, but you should only wear them for your husband after you are married. I regularly tell my wife as she heads into Victoria's Secret, "Spare no expense, and fill that little pink bag."

My young sisters in Christ, please heed this warning. I am not an old fuddy-duddy preacher. I regularly tell the young women in our church that what they wear speaks directly to their character. Let your closet reflect your love for Jesus.

Will She Be a Good Mom?

Does she want to be a mom? I had many good friends who married their high school sweethearts right out of high school and immediately started having children. One particular friend gave birth to her first child at age nineteen. She stayed in the same town we grew up in and kept many of her high school friends, who kept up their single, party lifestyle. Throughout her early twenties she went clubbing into the early morning hours and then came home to sleep it off. Her husband went to work early, leaving their toddler in the care of her hungover, half-asleep mom. Men need to leave the single lifestyle and create boundaries with family and friends in order to be a good husband and father. Young women must do the same.

Being a good mom starts with investing your energy in the raising of children. Such a woman of noble character will have children who rise up and call her blessed (Prov. 31:28).

Fox Alert: Mouthy, Moody, Immodest Women

If she can't control her tongue, flies off the handle at the slightest disagreement, and dresses like she's working a street corner, then look elsewhere for a wife.

His and Her Character
Does He or She Reflect the Sacrifice of Jesus?

"Be imitators of God, therefore, as dearly loved children" (Eph. 5:1). When you were growing up there were probably times when you wanted to be like your dad or mom. At the moment, my daughter and son both want to grow up and work at our church. It's like that country song says, "I've been watching you, Dad…. I'm your buckaroo, I wanna be like you. And eat all my food and grow as tall as you are." My kids watch me every day and pick up on my life, good and bad. My kids and I will spend an average of three thousand hours a year together for the next several years. And children make great imitators. In many ways, children reflect their parents.

We are called to be imitators of our heavenly Father. We are His kids. The word in the Scriptures for "imitate Him" means to copy, to mimic, and to take on that life. Ephesians 5:2 says, "And live a life of love, just as Christ loved us and gave himself up for us as a fragrant offering."

Fragrance is a sign that the offering was acceptable. Over fifty times in the Old Testament we read about this idea of a fragrant offering in which the smell would either please God or displease God. In Malachi 1, we read about these sacrifices in which the priest would go out and find the most defective lamb. The priest would look for the lamb leaning up against the fence, crippled; the lamb that would probably be dead in a couple of weeks. Then he would bring this lamb as a sacrifice—and the Scriptures actually say that he brought the sacrifice in contempt. The fragrance of this sacrifice displeased God. The priest might as well have not have offered the sacrifice in the first place. He might as well have just shut the doors of the temple because it was not a pleasing, fragrant offering. What Christ did on the cross was a pleasing and fragrant offering to God, and He calls us to be similarly pleasing.

Romans 12:1 is the most often quoted challenge to live this pleasing offering: "Therefore, I urge you, brothers, in view of God's mercy, to offer your bodies as living sacrifices, holy and pleasing to God—this is your spiritual act of worship."

Norma Smalley calls this process "sniffing." She loves meeting with people and having her "sniffer" in high gear. You must smell your potential spouse's aroma. Is he or she a pleasing offering to God?

Is He or She Committed to Purity While Dating and Engaged?

Your character must remain pure. Paul said, "But among you there must not be even a hint of sexual immorality" (Eph. 5:3). You'll notice this verse tells us to stay away from sexual immorality altogether. Young adults who are dating always want to know, "How far can we go?" That's the wrong question to ask. What they're really asking is, "How far can we go in our dating relationship, physically, without getting in trouble?" Wrong emphasis. Wrong question.

I always love to tell young guys, "You treat her like a sister when you go out on a date. You treat her with the same kind of respect. If you kiss her, it'd better be like kissing your sister" (1 Tim. 5:1–2). You are more than welcome to kiss your sister on the cheek.

Here's my plan for Corynn's very first date. As I'm walking her and her date to the car, I will walk between them with my arms around them both. As we approach the car, I am going to kiss him right on the lips. And I mean a good one. Then I'm going to say, "Whatever you plan on doing with my daughter tonight, I will do to you when you get back. So you just keep that in the back of your mind."

As you live as an imitator of Christ, you must guard your love from lust.

Is He or She Greedy?

Guard your lives from "any kind of impurity, or of greed, because these are improper for God's holy people" (Eph. 5:3). The two primary stumbling blocks of believers in the church today are sex and money. These sins can get a hold of our lives. Sex and money are not bad or evil. However, when we pervert sex and love money, we get into trouble and lose our integrity.

Greed destroys marriages when young couples start to spend more money than they make. In most young marriages, income is low, but a couple's lifestyle can quickly get out of control when high expectations cause overspending.

Debt is stressful. It places a couple under bondage and builds their hatred toward God: "No one can serve two masters. Either he will hate the one and love the other, or he will be devoted to the one and despise the other. You cannot serve both God and Money" (Matt. 6:24).

Does His or Her Mouth Reflect Christ?

"Nor should there be obscenity, foolish talk or coarse joking, which are out of place, but rather thanksgiving" (Eph. 5:4). When we open our mouths, we should reflect the sacrifice of Christ. The Bible teaches us that our words flow from our hearts, so if you want to know about a person's character, listen to his or her words. The tongue will tell all:

> We all stumble in many ways. If anyone is never at fault in what he says, he is a perfect man, able to keep his whole body in check.
>
> When we put bits into the mouths of horses to make them obey us, we can turn the whole animal. Or take ships as an example. Although they are so large and are driven by strong winds, they are steered by a very small rudder wherever the pilot wants to go. Likewise the tongue is a small part of the body, but it makes great boasts. Consider what a great

forest is set on fire by a small spark. The tongue also is a fire, a world of evil among the parts of the body. It corrupts the whole person, sets the whole course of his life on fire, and is itself set on fire by hell. (James 3:2–6)

Do His or Her Closest Friends Reflect Christ?

You and I both know the difference between the friends and the associates who influence us and those we influence. My friend Rick Rigsby loves to tell young people, "If you are the strongest follower of Christ among your friends, then you need new friends." We all tend to take on the lifestyles and patterns of those we hang around with on a regular basis. We get our jokes from them. We get our language from them.

So now what? Do I cut myself off from the world? No. Jesus encouraged His disciples to be friends with sinners, and Jesus was a friend of sinners. But there is a difference between friendship for the purpose of leading the person to Jesus, and being a partner in crime, so to speak. Paul said, "Do not be partners" (Eph. 5:7) with those who lead you *away* from Christ. So where are your intimate friends and associates right now? Are they leading you toward the world, or are they leading you toward Christ? What do your close friends say about your character?

Premarital Counseling

Do you want your parents, family, and friends to take your young marriage seriously? Prove it with your character. Paul told young

Timothy not to let anyone look down on him because of his young age. He challenged Timothy to "set an example for the believers in speech, in life, in love, in faith and in purity" (1 Tim. 4:12). Similarly, the way you talk, model mature behaviors, love others, believe, and commit to sexual purity screams, "I can be taken seriously!" Make sure that everything about your life models the gospel. If you've been dating someone who reflects Jesus in his or her speech, life, love, faith, and purity, then I counsel you to get married. Money, compatibility, and irreconcilable differences are common answers couples use to justify divorce. You rarely ever hear integrity used as a reason for divorce. Most spouses will walk away from their marriage because they lack character, but don't let that be you. Do not marry someone with a low level of character and integrity.

It would have served Amy and me well to bring a professional tree inspector out to check out the hollow tree on our property. We did everything else right. We maintained our budget, hit deadlines, and completed a beautiful home. Had we consulted a general contractor, someone with more experience and better understanding of the building process, we could have saved time, money, and heartache.

You need an inspector too. Get a pastor, counselor, Bible study leader, elder, or deacon to sit down with you and your boyfriend or girlfriend and inspect your character. Your "tingles" bring you too close to the forest to see the trees. You need the advice of someone who is objective and not easily impressed to help you discern the right decision. If either one of you resists this kind of scrutiny, then that's a huge red flag! Rejection of premarital counseling or advice from elders is often a sign of arrogance and can point to a lack of character.

A trusted man or woman of God will help ensure that you can wait for your spouse on your wedding day just as the Shullamite waited for Solomon. His character was the first attribute she called out as she saw him in the distance. As Solomon approached the Shullamite, she said, "Who is this coming up from the desert like a column of smoke, perfumed with myrrh and incense made from all the spices of the merchant?" (Song 3:6). The Shullamite used a powerful word picture from the Old Testament to speak of her groom's character.

The children of Israel wandered in the wilderness for forty years. During that time, they were led by the Spirit of God, which was manifested in the form of a pillar of cloud by day and a pillar of fire by night. So here we see an allusion to the Spirit of God in this passage from Song of Songs. Also, the knitting of this couple by almighty God surely received public recognition on the day of their wedding. In other words, their wedding pointed to God's Spirit, which led them to that day, and in that they acknowledged that God was the author of their relationship.

Marriage is a sacred covenant that is a legal, public, and binding agreement. Just as you wouldn't sign on the dotted line if you knew the car salesman was shady, you most definitely shouldn't sign if you think the one you are marrying is hollow in character. A used car you can trade in after a few years. Marriage is a lifetime.

Check out www.youngandinlove.com for video podcasts, articles, and resources to help you prepare for marriage.

Young and in Love Marriage Journal

Is he a one-woman man?

Is he a hard worker?

Does he submit well to authority?

Is he easily angered?

Will he be a great dad?

Is he too attached to his mom, hobbies, or friends?

Is she a busybody or malicious talker?

Is she moody?

Is she modest?

Will she be a good mom?

Does he or she reflect the sacrifice of Jesus?

Is he or she committed to purity while dating and engaged?

Is he or she greedy?

Does his or her mouth reflect Christ?

Do his or her closest friends reflect Christ?

Fox Alert: Avoidance

Do you get any serious reaction to the journal questions? If so, you need to work through them and get below the surface a bit more. This is where a pastor or trusted counselor can really help. Trained leaders often know when someone is trying to dodge a question. Avoiding a direct answer to a question usually means someone is trying to hide something (many politicians have mastered this strategy).

Chapter 9

Chemistry

My dove in the clefts of the rock, in the hiding places on
the mountainside, show me your face, let me hear your
voice; for your voice is sweet, and your face is lovely.

—Song of Songs 2:14

Do opposites attract? Should I look for compatibility? How do we
weigh all of our likes and dislikes? Which are more important, similarities or differences, when it comes to finding "the one"?

All of these questions are secondary to the character questions
we covered in the last chapter. Faith, purity, integrity, and commitment trump the pursuit of chemistry and compatibility every
time. Finding the right match is less complicated than we like to
make it:

The chemistry challenge affects all ages and all couples and
seems to be one of the most frequently given reasons for the failure

of young marriages. When I meet with a young woman in her early twenties seeking a divorce, the dialogue usually goes something like this.

"He's changed," she says.

"How so?" I ask.

"He's just not the same guy I married," she insists.

Eventually she tells me that he's changed in many different ways, but the reasons are usually simple: First, he may be growing up and accepting more responsibility—in which case he may not seem as fun as when she first met him. He's moving away from too much privilege and embracing responsibility. That probably speaks more of her character, resistance to change, and desire not to grow up rather than of his character.

Second, he may not be changing at all but now she's just seeing more of who he really is. In which case she is being asked to accept more of him, with his secrets and all. And again that speaks to her maturity, not her compatibility with her husband.

I hope both people change when they get married. Growth is something a couple *should* experience over a lifetime. The most extreme case of the chemistry challenge I deal with occurs when two people marry as non-Christians, and then one spouse commits his or her life to Christ. That's a bigger challenge than a Baptist marrying a charismatic or a Methodist marrying a Presbyterian. A Christian and a non-Christian together present the issue of an unequally yoked and therefore mismatched marriage. In that situation, the Bible clearly teaches that the believer should not leave the unbeliever; instead he or she should stay and be a godly witness to his or her spouse (1 Cor. 7:12–14; 1 Peter 3:1–6).

If God does not expect a married Christian to leave a non-Christian, all other forms of chemistry change in a relationship seem trivial by comparison. You need to plan for your chemistry changing and for your life taking on added pressures. Children, homes, bills, church, friends, in-laws, and jobs all affect a couple's chemistry. As these new elements are added to the situation, try to keep the fundamentals from your dating years alive.

Much of the dating experience is concerned with *curiosity* and *fascination*. You spend countless hours getting to know the one you love, asking great questions, and diving deep into issues of the heart. In the Song of Songs, King Solomon painted a wonderful word picture of this stage of love:

> My dove in the clefts of the rock,
> in the hiding places on the mountainside,
> show me your face,
> let me hear your voice;
> for your voice is sweet,
> and your face is lovely. (Song 2:14)

Solomon was saying here, "I want to get to know you." He loved it when she spoke and shared herself with him, and he wanted to communicate with her. As you discover new elements in your marriage chemistry, continue to live in awe and fascination of each other rather than in judgment.

Chances are good that you will marry someone very different from you. You will likely respond to situations and people in a much different way than your spouse does. However, when you understand the way you and your spouse are hardwired, you can recover from escalated arguments quicker and establish longer-lasting harmony.

Most of the couples I meet in counseling struggle to find common ground in their differences. Remember, the differences often lay dormant during the dating years and only surface after you begin experiencing tension through the mundane activities of life. We work with a lot of couples by getting both of them to understand the natural personality of their mate. At the same time each person must resist the temptation to change the way God made his or her spouse. Instead we encourage couples to begin bringing balance to their own personality while finding ways of accepting their mate's.

The Four Personalities

Most people tend to be a blend of two or more of the four basic personality types.[1] They may have one dominant personality trait, but it's usually combined with a second type. No matter what the personality combinations are in your marriage, you can learn skills to enjoy a happy, fruitful, and satisfying marriage. And learning about these personality types on the front side of marriage can save a lot of heartache.

The Precise Personality

The Precise Personality loves numbers and making things work right. This person pays attention to statistics and enjoys keeping a budget and balancing the checkbook. The Precise Personality loves measuring and comparing things, and most issues are clearly black or white. He or she is constantly evaluating incoming data and will happily tell you what you've done wrong and, usually, how you can do it better. Precise Personalities help organizations run effectively and efficiently.

They value accuracy, details, correctness, and discernment. They are often great listeners. If they're not careful, they can be too critical and controlling in their pursuit of perfection. When someone withholds details, they assume that person is lying.

If you're considering marrying a Precise Personality, plan on giving them as many details as possible. Even when you think the details are unnecessary, give them anyway because it shows them that you care.

The Pleaser Personality

The Pleaser Personality is warm and relational and tends to be extremely loyal. This personality type maintains a sense of calm in the most stressful of situations and has a knack for being a natural peacemaker. The Pleaser Personality is often concerned with group dynamics and the atmosphere of the room. More than anything, he or she wants to make sure everyone and everything is good.

The world is a better place because of Pleaser Personalities. They tend to be the glue that holds people and organizations together. They are quick to welcome, serve, and embrace others, and they value peace, loyalty, and routine. If they aren't careful they can be easily hurt. They tend to take things too personally.

If you plan on marrying a Pleaser Personality, be cautious of his or her feelings. Pleaser Personalities can be taken advantage of, so you must work at valuing their loyalty. If your spouse does not embrace all of your friends, it's not because he or she thinks your friends are bad people. Pleaser Personalities prefer to go deep with fewer people instead of going shallow with a lot of people. So don't expect your spouse to be a party mixer.

The Party Personality

Party Personalities are all about fun and will cheer you on in your activities. Right before participating in a dangerous activity they'll usually say, "Hey, watch this." They love attention.

Party Personalities are always on the go, ready to try a new sport, jump out of a plane, or catch a concert—*at the very last minute*. Along the way, they'll make sure the laughter is loud and everyone gets to hear some of their best stories. They are extreme optimists, very energetic, daydreamers, and fantastic motivators. They're constantly imagining what could be, as well as how much fun it could be! They tend to come up with great ideas and love to be spontaneous.

Unfortunately, as enjoyable as Party Personalities are to be around, they also have their blind spots—like when it comes to doing the work needed to throw the party. Though they may love being the center of attention at the party, that doesn't mean they should be the ones throwing the party! Their organizational skills often leave much to be desired, and all their excitement can be overbearing. While they have a lot to say when it comes to making a decision, they may be too busy to actually follow through.

If you plan on marrying a Party Personality, be careful not to take everything so seriously. We could all stand to lighten up a bit, and the Party Personality reminds us to do just that. Avoid belittling this personality with constant words like, "Come on, get serious!" or "Why don't you ever take things seriously?"

The Powerful Personality

Powerful Personalities love making decisions. They are task oriented and focus on getting things done. This happens to be my personality. Powerful Personalities naturally step up to leadership opportunities. They're quick to take the reins of a project or activity, and they aren't afraid of competition or confrontation.

Powerful Personalities tend to look at relationships as *I'm your coach, not your friend.* They tend to have high expectations of themselves and others. They are not afraid to speak up, and they're willing to do what it takes to make sure the job gets done.

If left unchecked, the Powerful Personality has a natural tendency to think, *It's my way or the highway.* As a result, he or she can undermine relationships within a community or work environment. If a Powerful Personality gets out of balance, he or she may use his or her gung ho leadership skills to mow over or intimidate others. The result can be a lot of relational damage.

If you plan on marrying a Powerful Personality, then remember to save money for counseling. I'm just kidding, *sort of.* My most difficult counseling appointments have been with a husband and wife who both have a Powerful Personality. Talk about a battle of the wills. It's like putting two lions in a cage together, and it often seems as if only one will come out alive.

Honor the Differences

Remember, you do not have the best personality type. They're all great! Realize that you are truly different from your spouse—and that's a good thing! Take a moment to read through the words of Psalm 139:13–16:

For you created my inmost being;
> you knit me together in my mother's womb.

I praise you because I am fearfully and wonderfully
made;
> your works are wonderful,
>
> I know that full well.

My frame was not hidden from you
> when I was made in the secret place.

When I was woven together in the depths of the
earth,
> your eyes saw my unformed body.

All the days ordained for me
> were written in your book
>
> before one of them came to be.

When you honor and esteem someone as a unique creation and highly valuable, you cannot help but transform your relationship with that person for the better. Honoring someone is simply seeing him or her as personally autographed by God. Romans 15:7 tells us, "Accept one another, then, just as Christ accepted you, in order to bring praise to God." In other words, God is pleased when you honor others and yourself.

Precise Personality, remember that you sometimes may have to move forward in life without figuring everything out perfectly. You may need to complete a project or a household chore even though it's not perfect. Even when it feels uncomfortable, you need to risk and even embrace adventure. Don't expect your spouse to share every detail of the day. And by all means, remember that he or she is not lying when some details get left unsaid. Stretch yourself by not taking yourself or life too seriously.

Pleaser Personality, you must be careful not to wear your heart on your sleeve. People, including your mate, may take advantage of that, whether unconsciously or not. Release past hurts and let your spouse off the hook for past mistakes. Learn to make decisions in the midst of uncertainty about what is best for everyone. Branch out and meet new people.

Party Personality, learn to follow through on your ideas and especially your commitments. If you go to Lowe's and buy tools to do a project around the house, then complete the project. If you don't follow through, you'll drive the Precise Personality nuts and frustrate the Powerful Personality. Remember: Just because the fun leaves the project doesn't mean the project is over.

Powerful Personality, learn to add softness. Study ways to become a better listener and realize that not every statement needs a response. Tame your words with love, and temper your tone with gentleness. Look for opportunities to take other people's feelings into account.

Learning to honor personality differences takes time, especially in marriage. It doesn't happen overnight, and it will require numerous trial-and-error attempts to grow closer before it actually begins to work. You may think you're doing something your spouse would love, when in fact it's driving your spouse nuts! Those moments will become scrapbook memories that can provide lots of laughter in the years to come (though it probably isn't funny in the moment).

Ephesians 4:2 tells us, "Be completely humble and gentle; be patient, bearing with one another in love." When you practice that verse in a marriage, your relationship cannot help but grow stronger. At the same time, you'll find the gap between your personalities shrinking as you learn to love each other more deeply.

I want to work every day to bring balance to my personality. I don't want it to be out of balance. I don't want to be known as someone who is pushy, obnoxious, or demanding, and I don't want to be a bad listener. Who wants that label? No one! That's why we need to learn to seek that balance—to grow in humility, gentleness, patience, and love. In fact, when the fruit of the Spirit is nurtured in our lives, we can't help but become more gracious to others.

Sleeping Beauty, Cinderella, and Snow White went through some tough times before they got their happily-ever-afters. And guess what? Your marriage will go through ups and downs too.

Most of us come into adulthood with a distorted vision of a healthy love relationship. Our models of love often come from songs, books, friends, movies, or television, some of which depict love as fast blooming, overwhelming, intense, romantic, and always requited. But these models display only one stage of love, the very first stage of infatuation, which is caused by chemistry. Good marriages contain many more elements than simple infatuation, yet the lovers in many of our books and movies never get far enough into the stories for us to see those elements unfold. We usually don't know whether the lovers stayed together long enough to determine if they were committed for the long term. We see an hour and a half of two people facing misunderstanding and frustration until they go off romantically into the sunset. We never get to see what happens next.

These images of love leave us with serious misconceptions about what constitutes a relationship, such as:

- Passion equals love.
- My lover should meet all my needs and make me happy.
- Once love dies, you can't get it back.
- Chemistry is all that matters.
- Love conquers all.
- When things get tough, it means you have the wrong partner.
- Once you're in love, you stay on a high forever.
- Love is a feeling, and you either have it or you don't.

These are all lies or, at best, gross misunderstandings of the true nature of love. Eventually, all marriages come off the high of infatuation, but that does not mean love is dead. Not at all! In fact, it may be just the beginning. True love learns to be gentle, humble, and honoring when someone rubs you the wrong way.

Powerful vs. Pleaser

I am the powerful, and Amy is the pleaser. The differences in our personalities almost prevented our marriage from ever occurring. We never had doubts about marriage until we went on a mission trip to Mexico in the spring of 1996.

I led a group of ten college students on a trip to remodel an orphanage outside Mexico City. Once we arrived on site at the orphanage, we had five days to buy supplies, construct a few major walls, build a bathroom, drywall, tape, mud, and paint a total of five rooms. Granted, for nonskilled students, myself included, that's a lot of work to accomplish in a few short days. Projects like these are perfect for the Powerful Personality, but it can be miserable for the ones participating.

We were making good progress on the building when on day three one of our students approached me with a request that he tried to pass off as a statement.

"Hey, Ted," Tony began. "I talked to a few guys from our group, and we decided to take the day off and head to town for a little fun."

Tony was the oldest student in our group, and in my opinion he had prolonged his adolescence too much already. He was ten years older than me, and immediately I was ready to mow him over. He was a fun guy, but work and responsibility were not his strong suit.

"Tony, if we take the day off, we will leave the project unfinished," I responded.

With that I got up from breakfast and began feverishly working, alone. Amy came up and asked me what was going on. I stayed silent. Inside, I was furious with Tony and felt ready to explode, so in order to keep my cool, I withdrew and kept my mouth shut.

This was the first time Amy saw me in a leadership role, and she felt shocked when she saw me put Tony in his place. In my opinion, though, we were in Mexico to work, not play, and the fun would come after the job was done. Later, I gathered the group, gave my little lecture, and got everybody back to work.

When we finished working that day, Amy and I found ourselves sitting on an old couch on the rooftop of the orphanage. I could tell she was considering ending our relationship, and we talked for a long time. Things were touch and go, but I reminded her that mutiny was averted. The day had been a shock, giving her a glimpse into what she would have to deal with in marrying a pastor, marrying me.

We all need to learn balance. And although I still have times when I am out of balance as a leader, Amy graciously sees it as the way God made me. She does not want to change me as she did when we first were married.

Chemistry still plays into our marriage. When Amy and I want to grab a bite to eat, I'll ask her where she wants to go, and once in a blue moon she'll have a strong opinion. Usually, she's happy with anything. The only time she really disagrees is when we head to the same restaurant for the twelfth consecutive time. Powerful Personalities love routine. So she reminds me that we're falling into a rut, and I need that reminder!

Check out www.youngandinlove.com for video podcasts, articles, and resources to help you prepare for marriage.

Young and in Love Marriage Journal

Which personality best describes you?

Which personality best describes the person you are dating or marrying?

What is it going to take to match your personalities?

What do you foresee as the greatest "rub" or source of tension?

Are you prepared for the inevitable changes that you
and your spouse will experience in marriage? What can
you do now to prepare yourself?

Fox Alert: Duty and Responsibility

Do not allow duty and responsibility to trump curiosity and fascination in your marriage. If you're not careful you will use paying the bills, going out with friends, or working a job as an excuse to maintain the vacuum of intimacy you have allowed into your marriage. Continue to ask your spouse great questions.

Chapter 10

Competency

I [God] have filled him with ... skill, ability
and knowledge in all kinds of crafts.

—Exodus 31:3

Michael believes working at a movie theater or in fast food is beneath him. He's sixteen years old, and he's holding out for the more lucrative position with a nice benefits package. Shane started his own company at the age of twelve and now nets $1,500 per month selling T-shirts online. He's nineteen years old and paying his own way through college. Sarah's dad told her that she would need to get a job in college to learn responsibility. Dad pays for her tuition, room, board, books, car payments, insurance, and gas. Sarah works only for extra spending money. Leighann attends College of the Ozarks, where she takes fifteen credit hours of classes per semester and works fifteen hours per week to cover her tuition and an additional twenty hours off campus to cover her other expenses. She is twenty-one years old.

I love this C!

I love encouraging young couples to get creative and find unique ways to make a living in the early years of their marriage. For most young people I work with today, I am the first one to picture a special future for them. After childhood dreams of making it to the NFL or NBA, or as a fashion designer in New York City do not pan out, parents usually send their kids off to college. But most young people are sent into the world with few job skills and low earning potential. And when you grow up with too much privilege, the responsibility wake-up call can be brutal. Competency is the measure of your skills, their future potential for income, and the number of opportunities available to you.

Rick and Kim

Rick lived in Illinois and Kim in Missouri. He was a hardworking blue-collar guy, and Kim was a successful ministry leader. They fell in love and planned to get married, but there were complications. Several members of Kim's board expressed concern that she was getting into a bad marriage. This was not Kim's first marriage, and they were concerned that she was setting herself up for a failure by rushing into this marriage.

I was called into a meeting with Kim and two members from her board. Since all three of them were members of my church and I'd been a part of Kim's premarital counseling, I looked forward to the opportunity to help. Apparently, Kim and one of her ministry board members had tried to talk about the upcoming marriage at a recent lunch appointment, and the meeting had come to a head. They needed a mediator.

As we opened the meeting, the tension in the room was thick. Everyone felt the big pink elephant in the room, so I called it by name.

"Why shouldn't Kim marry Rick?" I asked.

"Ted, I do not want to see Kim fail again, and I feel as though she is allowing her strong desire to have a man in her life cloud her judgment," one of the board members responded.

The heart behind her answer conveyed a clear love for Kim, and I saw no hidden agendas or egos in her answer. After a few minutes of back-and-forth and validating the feelings of everyone involved, I asked permission to walk the group through the four Cs as a framework. I had already walked Kim and Rick through the Cs and was on board with their marriage, but I needed to help the group better understand the decision. The group agreed to the exercise.

On a whiteboard in the corner of the room, I wrote four simple words:

Character, Chemistry, Competency, Calling.

I knew Rick was being called into question by the board members, so I had to answer for him in his absence. I started by asking a question: "Is there anything in Rick's character that we need to call into question? Is he a deeply committed follower of Jesus? Does he have any addictions that we need to discuss? Is he an angry person? Is he a hard worker?"

We all sighed and put a check next to *Character.* I was relieved. The more we talked about him, the more we all liked him. So I continued.

"Next, chemistry. Kim, do you get along well? What are the conflicts?"

We spent a few minutes going over Kim's strong Powerful Personality and Rick's Pleaser Personality and the struggles they would need to overcome, but both board members saw no biblical reason having to do with chemistry to keep these two from marrying. We put a check next to *Chemistry,* and we were halfway home.

Competency threw us a curveball.

One of the board members spoke up and said, "Ted, I am just going to say it. There will be problems with Kim as a well-educated woman marrying an uneducated guy. This is going to pose some problems that Kim is not thinking through." This was the sticking point for the board members, and Kim became quite emotional over this statement. And as a result, we spent the most time discussing this particular C. Kim was being accused of marrying down.

I made a strong appeal about the absence of biblical support to walk away from marriage based on the skill set or education of the potential spouse. However, competency does have many factors to consider.

Marrying someone with *specialized skills* may require a couple to move where the work is. Crab fishermen, marine biologists, ranchers, and park rangers are regionally limited in where their skills can be used. Some skill sets, such as those possessed by coaches, teachers, and law enforcement, have limited opportunities in a given location. In this case, Rick is skilled in upholstery, and Branson is a town of only six thousand people. Therefore, making money recovering furniture and car seats could be tough. Ultimately, this could affect Kim's job, and they might need to move so he can find work. Or he might need to learn a new set of skills.

However, marrying someone with multiple college degrees does not guarantee an income either. For example, it's easier to find work in Branson as someone with managerial skills rather than as someone who just received his bachelor's degree in psychology. The fact is that Rick may have a greater earning potential than Kim. If he learns new skills, he could make double what Kim makes as a leader of a nonprofit organization.

Marrying someone who has exceptional vocational skills but lacks in social skills may guarantee good income but create other struggles. I have a couple of doctor friends who perform intricate surgeries during the day but can be difficult to connect with over dinner.

Kim was marrying a competent guy who had specialized skills and the willingness to learn new ones. We put a check by this C. Much of our competency conversation bled over into the fourth C—*calling*.

The bottom line is at the end of our conversation, we ended up with four check marks. Rick and Kim sit on my right in the second row at Woodland Hills Family Church every Sunday morning. God has blessed their marriage, and we so love Rick that we employ him part-time at the church. He is skilled in many areas and serves on our maintenance team.

Amy and Me

Just like Kim's coworkers did, someone challenged my love for Amy over the C of competency. Never in my wildest dreams would I have considered walking away from her simply because she lacked computer skills. But that was the issue. Amy had so many wonderful qualities when we were dating, but apparently she didn't shine in the computer lab.

A professor and mentor of mine taught Liberty's most dreaded required class. No matter what he or she majored in, every student had to take Business 102. This class was an introduction to computers, word processing, and spreadsheets. At the time, we learned Lotus 1-2-3 and how to create a loan amortization schedule, which caused much angst and hindered many in their spiritual growth. Many ministry majors lost their progressive sanctification over this class. But I loved it. Especially when I learned how much interest accrues on a home loan. And that many times you actually spend more on interest than you do on the price of a home. Very disturbing!

After I completed Business 102, my professor asked me to become a tutor for the class, and I jumped at the opportunity. Within a year, I was leading the tutors and running the computer labs for academic computing.

Amy waited until her junior year to take this dreaded class, which was perfect because by that point I got to be her tutor. She received extra special attention. But it took only a few weeks for the professor to realize that Amy had no passion or enthusiasm for his class. This led him to sit me down for a father-son talk.

"Ted, I understand you are pretty serious about Amy Freitag?" he inquired.

"Serious? I plan on marrying her," I responded.

He paused. I could tell he had something difficult to say but was struggling with the words.

"You do know she is not all that interested in my class?" he continued.

"Yes, along with the majority of the student body," I said with respect and sarcasm mixed together. I could tell where he was headed, but I didn't think he would try to discourage our marriage because she hated doing formulas in Lotus 1-2-3. I was wrong. He went there.

"You need to think this through, Ted," he encouraged me, which was his way of saying, "Ted, you so enjoy spreadsheets—how can you be with someone who doesn't?"

I left the room without saying anything further, and we didn't discuss the subject for the rest of my senior year.

When Amy and I first got married, I was a bivocational pastor. Our friend who set us up on our first date graduated from Liberty a year before me and became the pastor of Southside Baptist Church in Lakeland, Georgia. He offered me a job as his associate but was able to pay me only ten thousand dollars a year. I knew that my calling was as a pastor, but the pay was not enough to cover the bills. I knew I had to get another job to get Amy and me started in life as well as fulfill my call to ministry.

I was given the opportunity to become a teacher but instead chose to be a systems administrator at a Lowe's Distribution Center. The only reason I went the technology route was time and money. I needed a full-time job that did not require weekends or evenings and that paid well. I wanted to make the most money possible while leaving plenty of time to serve in my role at the church. Programming computers was not high on my list—I found that I hated it—but I'd picked up the skill in college to make a few extra bucks.

Amy has a ton of skills that have provided for us over the years. While in Georgia she worked at a Christian bookstore. She also has a passion for interior decorating. She has an eye for the way a room should look. She turned that into contract work hanging borders, wallpapering homes, and painting. Extra income like this was always nice, especially early on.

Why is competency a part of our premarital counseling at Woodland Hills? I have two answers to that question: *hope* and *whining*.

Skilled labor generally has a higher value than hard labor. The more skills you have, the more attractive you are to future employers. I want young couples to have hope, when they first get married, that they can earn plenty of money in lots of different ways.

I hate whining. I got a Facebook message once from a college student asking me if the church could help him with his rent. I replied by asking this single young man if he worked forty hours a week, and I never heard back from him.

On the road to responsibility I don't think young people should have to call home for help with rent. Get creative, and pick up a temp job to make it through. Go to a temp agency on your day off to earn an extra hundred dollars. Find seasonal employment a day or two a week during peak season. There are hundreds of ways to make money. If necessary, learn a new skill that makes you more marketable to potential employers. Try new things. "I can't" or "I don't know how" do not fly. If you try it and fail, that's okay. But at least give it a shot. Work a mind-numbing job to provide for your family, but always have ambition for something more. Never stop learning or working.

Amy and I have been married now for fourteen years, and I've been bivocational almost the whole time. To this day, I am a pastor, writer, and speaker, and in seminary I held down three different jobs. I took three classes a semester, worked as a network administrator at a civil-engineering firm, led worship at a church on weekends, and worked from home doing light programming for a Bible website. You may be judging me for being money hungry, but I loved paying cash for my seminary tuition.

I believe that both skilled labor and working more than one job is very biblical. Jesus was a trained carpenter, and the apostle Paul was a tentmaker. Paul made tents so he could live out his calling as we see in Acts: "Paul went to see them, and stayed and worked with them, because he earned his living by making tents, just as they did. He held discussions in the synagogue every Sabbath, trying to convince both Jews and Greeks" (Acts 18:2–4 GNT).

Cowboy Scotty and His Two Wives

On a recent speaking trip my family and I went horseback riding through Rocky Mountain National Park in Estes Park, Colorado. Our family intrigued our guide, a cowboy named Scotty, so he asked me the typical guy question: "What do you do for a living?"

"I'm a pastor," I said.

"That's cool," he responded. "What brings you guys to Estes?"

"I'm speaking at a men's conference a couple miles up the road," I answered.

"What do you speak on at a men's conference?" he asked.

"I'm speaking on marriage and what it takes to be a great husband," I said while he ponied my five-year-old's horse.

He continued to say, "Oh, marriage didn't really work for me. I tried it twice."

I said, "Scotty, you know what researchers are discovering? Marriage is not the cause of divorce."

He responded with, "I'm a cowboy, and I'll always be a cowboy. I can only marry someone who is willing to live with a cowboy."

I responded, "How can I pray for you, Scotty?"

Divorcing over occupation is just plain silly because marriage skills should always come before job skills. If necessary we must be willing to adjust what we do in the working world for the sake of our marriages. Jesus and Paul are great examples of working a job with seemingly no eternal value in order to fulfill an ultimate purpose of extreme eternal significance. Paul put it this way: "Work willingly at whatever you do, as though you were working for the Lord rather than for people" (Col. 3:23 NLT).

Check out www.youngandinlove.com for video podcasts, articles, and resources to help you prepare for marriage.

Young and in Love Marriage Journal

Take a look at the following skills and then sketch out a few ways you can turn your particular competencies into income, both in the long term and short term:

Entertaining: to perform, act, dance, speak, or do magic

Artistic: to conceptualize, picture, draw, paint, photograph, or make renderings

Graphics: to lay out, design, and create visual displays or banners

Planning: to strategize, design, and organize programs and events

Managing: to supervise people to accomplish a task and coordinate the details involved

Counseling: to listen, encourage, and guide with sensitivity

Teaching: to explain, train, demonstrate, or tutor

Writing: to write articles, letters, or books

Repairing: to fix, restore, or maintain

Feeding: to create meals for large or small groups of people

Mechanical: to operate equipment, tools, or machinery

Counting: to work with numbers, data, or money

Serving: to wait tables, make beds, or clean rooms

Public Relations: to handle complaints and customers with care and courtesy

Welcoming: to convey warmth, develop rapport, and make others feel comfortable

Landscaping: to garden and work with plants

Decorating: to beautify a setting for a special event

Maintain: to efficiently maintain something that is already organized

What is your plan for income and work early in your marriage?

If you are planning to continue college after marriage, how will that work?

Will your plans for marriage and education affect the
type of job you do? Why or why not?

Is relocation necessary to secure a job?

Fox Alert: Unemployment

One of my favorite Dave Ramsey quotes is when he tells young
people, "Out of all the millionaires I hang out with, not one of them
knows who got voted off the island." He is of course referring to the
reality show *Survivor* and the generational craze of reality TV. There
are a lot of ways to make money, and watching television is not one
of them, unless of course you're a third-shift security guard. Get out
there, get creative, and provide for your young marriage.

Chapter 11

Calling

I pray also that the eyes of your heart may be enlightened in order that
you may know the hope to which he has called you, the riches of his
glorious inheritance in the saints, and his incomparably great power for
us who believe. That power is like the working of his mighty strength.

—Ephesians 1:18-19

He is a gifted artist. She is headed to Argentina to serve on the mission field. Should they marry with two different callings?

I was asked this question while speaking at Liberty University a few years back. He was concerned that marriage would be a roadblock to God's individual calling on each of them. My first thought was, *Can't you do art anywhere?* I would think Argentina would be a fantastic place to jump-start your life as an artist. I could be wrong. But more important than this, I felt he needed a better understanding of calling.

Calling is an ambiguous word in our church vocabulary. We throw it around for just about anything we want to do or abstain from. All one has to say is, "I don't feel called," followed by fill-in-the-blank, and you are off the hook from working with the junior-high boys, or whatever.

Biblically, every believer is *called*. Single or married, if you are a Christian, you are called. Paul laid out calling theology this way: "I pray also that the eyes of your heart may be enlightened in order that you may know the hope to which he has called you" (Eph. 1:18). Calling is not something reserved for super-spiritual Christians. Your life, family, marriage, and vocation should proclaim the life and practices of Jesus in every pursuit. *That* is your primary calling.

When you begin to get this truth in your heart, it takes your life out of the mundane. This truth brings meaning to the job that you can't stand. When you get up in the morning and ask, "What's the purpose of this?" you now have an answer.

You are a minister in whatever career you choose. It doesn't matter whether you make widgets or sell real estate—you have been called. The danger of pride lurks when we take this idea of calling and restrict it to a few enlightened Christians. This flippant use of calling produces religious leaders with elitist attitudes. And don't forget, Jesus had a lot to say to religious leaders with elitist attitudes, and none of it was good. The entire model of New Testament ministry is that leaders are not above you. They don't have a calling that surpasses your calling.

The problem is that our world's values are the opposite of God's values. The world lacks any sense of what Scripture describes as "calling," or the perspective that God has called and equipped people to serve Him through their work in the world. Instead, our culture encourages us to climb a work/identity ladder that is ultimately self-serving and often self-destructive.

God calls us to a far more stable foundation for our significance. He wants us to establish our identity in the fact that we are His children, created by Him to carry out good works as responsible people in His kingdom (Eph. 2:10). This is our calling or vocation from God. According to Scripture, our calling:

- is irrevocable (Rom. 11:29)
- is from God; He wants us to share in Christ's glory (2 Thess. 2:14)
- is a function of how God designed us (Eph. 2:10)
- is an assurance that God will give us everything we need to serve Him, including the strength to remain faithful to Him (1 Cor. 1:7–9)
- is what we should be proclaiming as our true identity (1 Peter 2:5, 9)
- carries us through suffering (1 Peter 2:19–21)
- is rooted in peace, no matter the circumstances in which we find ourselves (1 Cor. 7:15–24)
- is focused on eternal achievements, not merely temporal ones (Phil. 3:13—4:1)

Above all else, believers are called to character development, service to others, and loyalty to God. These can be accomplished wherever we live or work and whatever our occupational status or position in society. If we pursue these goals, we can enjoy great satisfaction and significance.[1]

Marriage can turn the direction of your calling 180 degrees. God can use another person to direct you, ignite passion for life, and redirect your career plans. That's why you need to be reasonable with this final C. You don't have to decline a marriage proposal because your potential spouse has an opposite "calling" on his or her life. I am thankful Amy didn't walk away from me but allowed God to use her to blend our paths together.

My Calling and Amy

I was a government major at Liberty University with a strong passion for working in the "political machine" called Washington DC. I spent the first three years of college stacking the deck so I could land my dream internship. I took all the right classes; worked multiple political campaigns in Ohio, Tennessee, and Virginia; and even visited with many lobby groups as I prepared for my senior year of college.

In the fall of 1995, before Amy and I got really serious, I was invited to serve in a highly sought-after position with the United States Senate Republican Policy Committee under Senator Bob Nichols. This was *the* dream. For starters, it was a paid position, and those were rare. Second, the internship guaranteed me a job right out of college.

When I received the call, I was shocked at the answer that rolled off my tongue!

The young legislative executive was kind and proud to offer me the job: "Ted, we would like you to come to work for the United States Senate." You don't get offers like that every day. After sharing with me the terms and financial package, he waited for my response.

"I appreciate the opportunity, but at this time I will need to decline," I said with no hesitation. "I am headed in a different direction." I had no clue what the new direction would be but was pleased to wait and see how God would direct me in my senior year.

To be perfectly honest with you, I wanted to marry Amy Freitag in a bad kind of way. My choice was between Amy and the United States Senate. No contest! If I had left Liberty for a semester, she would have been gone. You can argue the sovereignty of God with me all day long, but remember, Liberty was a competitive dating scene.

The summer before Amy and I started really getting serious, she served in an impoverished village on the island of Moloka'i. I received several letters from her while she was there and knew that her heart was being directed toward missions. Her letters were filled with passion and vision for her life.

This flies in the face of today's pressure on young people. Most young people today are being told to get their careers going first. But one oversight of that advice is that God can use your spouse to help establish your personal career and calling. I put my career on hold for marriage, and I am so glad I did. Amy was part of that redirection.

What if we applied this "wait and get established" line of reasoning often used for marriage in the context of college? Most of my friends have a job and career in a field totally unrelated to their college degree. Between the ages of eighteen and twenty-four, we spent four years and a lot of money on an education that we weren't yet mature enough to choose. Would it stand to reason that we should wait to get established before we get educated in the field we settle into? No. College isn't wasted because we were not yet matured. You could argue that college actually plays a part in the maturing process.

The same could be said of marriage. While marriage is a far weightier decision than a college major, it's still a valuable aid in our maturing process. Amy and I are still growing, learning, and, yes, maturing.

Dr. James Merritt, pastor of First Baptist Church in Snellville, Georgia, came to campus a few weeks after I declined the position with the U.S. Senate. Amy and I started seriously dating around that weekend. Our campus pastor invited all of the resident assistants, prayer leaders, and spiritual-life directors to a Friday night and Saturday training where Dr. Merritt was the speaker. As I sat there a few rows behind Amy (she was sitting with her team), I listened as Dr. Merritt shared the life goals he had developed while he was in college. They lined up almost exactly with my goals: financial independence by age twenty-five and millionaire by age thirty. As he walked through his professional journey and how he became a pastor, I knew that night that I would be a public servant, but not in government. I shared with Amy that night that full-time church ministry was the new direction for my life.

Roger and Kari

Roger and Kari Gibson married young but had no idea where they would be on their twentieth anniversary. They were high school sweethearts and married in their early twenties. She was a public-school teacher, and he worked for a nonprofit family ministry. They tried all different types of ministries. He once thought he would be an author, then speaker, then small-business owner. She enjoyed teaching, published children's books, and loved being a mom.

Raising a family consumed Roger and Kari in the early years. But two years ago God birthed a vision in both of their hearts. They felt led to adopt baby Zoie from Ethiopia. My wife and I had the privilege of being in the room when Kari downloaded the first pictures of Zoie. The room was filled with screams, tears, hugs, and high fives. It was a great day.

Then came "gotcha" day, the day they went to meet Zoie and bring her home. The entire Gibson family flew to Ethiopia to pick her up, but problems arose. They had accidentally spelled Roger's name wrong. They had him down as Robert. This messed everything up and forced the family to stay in the country for two additional weeks.

During those two weeks Roger would walk the streets each day with his children, buying meals for people they met on the street. God did a work in the entire family, but it was so gradual they couldn't see it. He was calling them to a ministry of justice and mercy.

Since then I've watched the entire Gibson family welcome this sweet little African princess into their home and love her as their own. And I have also watched this family embrace a new direction for their lives. Kari started a blog (www.MyCrazyAdoption.com) that became her full-time job. She is now an advocate, counselor, and fund-raiser for families who are in the process of adopting. The Gibsons take countless missions trips every year and have completely changed their lifestyle to give more of their money to the poor.

Adopting Zoie was an adventure, but they had no idea that God would lead their entire family in a new direction. God works through couples in powerful ways. Similarly, your marriage may change the direction of your life and enhance the quality of your ministry. Solomon put it this way: "A cord of three strands is not quickly broken" (Eccl. 4:12).

Check out www.youngandinlove.com for video podcasts, articles, and resources to help you prepare for marriage.

Young and in Love Marriage Journal

Does your fiancé(e) or significant other have a vision for life? Do you?

What is your plan for that vision?

Is there a common direction you feel led together?

How will marriage benefit your vocational calling?

Fox Alert: Ministry

Pastor Bill Hybels once said, "Do not allow your work for God to destroy God's work in you." I had to learn early in ministry that even my work for God could destroy God's work in my marriage and family.

Chapter 12

First Signs of Trouble

Love seems the swiftest, but it is the slowest of all
growths. No man or woman really knows what perfect love
is until they have been married a quarter of a century.

—Mark Twain

Time magazine published an article in 2009 titled "For Worse, Then for Better: Why Facing Stressful Life Events Early in Coupledom Can Lead to Longevity." The article states that while "stressful life events often amplify a couple's problems ... and increase the likelihood of divorce, studies also show that hardship can have an upside. For some couples, it's protective, helping solidify their commitment into unshakeable us-vs.-the-world resolve."[1]

The article goes on to quote psychologist and marriage researcher William Doherty, who talks about why stressful events can result in a stronger marriage: A crisis "smashes the illusion of invulnerability, ...

[which] was going to go away anyway, and I don't think there's any great loss to it going away sooner rather than later."[2]

Marriage researcher and expert John Gottman believes there are two key predictors of a resilient relationship: mutual support and a willingness to sacrifice. Scott Stanley, director of the Center for Marital and Family Studies at the University of Denver, and his colleagues found that the willingness to forgo personal interests and put a partner's needs ahead of one's own was directly linked to a long-lasting, happy marriage—provided that the sacrifices were not damaging or one-directional.[3]

Young and old marriages alike will face struggles, pain, and conflict. The longevity and marital satisfaction you experience as a couple is up to you. It has nothing to do with your age and everything to do with how you maturely process the pain you will face together.

Work on Your Character before Your Happiness

The Bible tells us that Solomon was the wisest man who walked the earth. He had knowledge and insights into everything—from how to manage money to how to maintain a great marriage. And he shared his wisdom with us in the books of Ecclesiastes and the Song of Songs. One of my favorite Solomonisms comes from Ecclesiastes 7:3, which says, "Sorrow is better than laughter, because a sad face is good for the heart." That may seem a little depressing at first, but here's what Solomon was really saying: *Pain shapes us.* God can use pain to mold us into His image and allow the fruit of the Spirit to grow in our lives in a fuller measure.

Marriage is the best tool I know of for making us more like Jesus because marriage builds character through patience and endurance.

Character cannot be built overnight and neither can your marriage. Think in terms of years, not weeks or months. It takes a lifetime. No one on earth will ever know you better than your spouse, so he or she must be a partner in your character development. Your spouse helps you quickly identify the chinks in your armor. Your spouse may be able to point out your character defects, but you are the only one who can change those defects. Always choose character even when it leads you down a difficult or painful road. People who are constantly looking for the easy way out are not going to become all that God created them to be.

Have you ever watched a marathon? The starting line is packed with people ready to run. In some of the larger races, such as the Boston Marathon, the race field looks like a sea of people. But what happens around mile twenty? The sea of people becomes like water droplets here and there as the runners thin out. Those who looked fresh in the beginning now look worn out. Some walk. Some aren't even in the race anymore.

Starting something new is easy. Anyone can start a new job or a new project. I'm particularly guilty of this because starting a project around the house is easy. Finishing it, well, that's a whole different matter.

Being a newlywed comes easily and naturally for many couples. In the beginning, the passion is easy and the intimacy is amazing because the relationship is blossoming. Fast-forward twenty or thirty years. What does the couple's marriage look like now? Are they still in love? Have they been able to weather tough economic times, job losses, parenting, and the death of loved ones—and still cherish one another?

Take the Good with the Bad

"Feast or famine!" That was our budgeting scenario in the first ten years of our marriage. Sometimes we had money to splurge on a vacation, and sometimes we didn't; but early on, we weren't ashamed to have some of our furniture held up by egg crates. The typical start to a marriage is in the "low funds" category. When it comes to good times and bad times, I immediately think of both the times of plenty *and* the times of want.

One of the primary reasons given for divorce is money. But I have news for you: Money does not cause divorce, and money is *not* the root of all evil. It is the love of money that is evil. Just remember, when you say for richer or for poorer, you'll probably start off poor.

In the Old Testament, Job had good times. He had a family, land, assets, and his health. But in the greatest test of his life, his faith was challenged. After losing his children, his property, and his health (which I would call bad times), his wife was done. She could not understand the test and begged her husband to give up and die: "His wife said to him, 'Are you still holding on to your integrity? Curse God and die!' He replied, 'You are talking like a foolish woman. Shall we accept good from God, and not trouble?' In all this, Job did not sin in what he said" (Job 2:9–10).

Will your marriage balance the good times and the bad times? Will you allow trouble to bring you closer together or push you further apart?

Work on Your Own Character, Not Your Spouse's

You can change your own expectations and 100 percent of yourself, but you cannot change all of your reality on your own, and that includes your spouse. I suggest you start this process by answering these questions: Do I need to change or adjust my expectations? Which of my expectations are reasonable or unreasonable? Which are based on biblical truth and which are not?

You are responsible for your heart, moods, words, and expectations in your relationship. Resolve not to force your mate to change because you will find that letting your mate off the hook will change the atmosphere of your marriage and home. Not only will you walk lighter, but your spouse will too. The goal of this shift is for you and your spouse to be able to sit down together and create new, realistic, and biblical expectations for the future.

"The Serenity Prayer" by Reinhold Niebuhr reminds us that we do not need to be in control of everything around us, including people, places, and things:

> God grant me the serenity
> to accept the things I cannot change;
> courage to change the things I can;
> and wisdom to know the difference.
> Living one day at a time;
> Enjoying one moment at a time;
> Accepting hardships as the pathway to peace;
> Taking, as He did, this sinful world
> as it is, not as I would have it;
> Trusting that He will make all things right
> if I surrender to His Will;
> That I may be reasonably happy in this life
> and supremely happy with Him

Forever in the next.

Amen.

On our wedding days, many of us have a fairy-tale world in our minds, a happily-ever-after story that we will be a part of, with no problems, disagreements, or concerns. The key to resolving the pain that comes when these expectations aren't met is not to try to adjust the behavior of your mate but rather to take personal responsibility for your expectations. Then you can bring your expectations into harmony with your mate's expectations. You will both discover that when you love each other and strive to become a "married team," you will adjust your expectations to be in sync with reality, and you will experience greater commitment to each other.

It's the gap between what you expect and what you actually experience that can drain your energy. To reduce this stress, together you can make a list of all of your recalled expectations and start figuring out how to reduce the gap between those expectations and reality. As you begin to understand God's expectations for you and your marriage, His Spirit will reveal areas that require change and will convict you of the need to change. Remember, you cannot change your spouse, but God gives you the power to change yourself. You can trust God and believe that He works in the lives of others to grow and change them in ways that you cannot.

Some of the highest expectations we hold are for ourselves. I know that when I don't meet my own expectations, I'm always tempted to belittle myself with negative self-talk. But what I've found is that I need to take a different approach. I've begun recognizing those moments as opportunities to celebrate my weaknesses.

Scripture reminds us, "My grace is sufficient for you, for my power is made perfect in weakness" (2 Cor. 12:9). Our weaknesses are an opportunity for God to be glorified. In fact, God's strength is made perfect when I am weak. When I realize this, then I can approach my shortcomings in a healthy way.

Whenever I place my expectations at the feet of Jesus, I can let go of the little things and focus on Him instead. I still have huge expectations, but now they are all on "things above, not on earthly things" (Col. 3:2). I love seeing God's faithfulness at work within me as I rest in Him and His words through the power of His Spirit. This is not a "pipe dream" expectation; this has become reality for me. He's my life. About one hundred of His most important Bible verses have become branded upon my heart through memorization, and I meditate on them several times a day. Nothing has changed me more and given me more fulfillment than meditating on His words and resting in Him daily for all the life I'll ever need.

Don't Quit

I want to be clear that when I say, "Resolve to stay," I'm not talking about staying in an abusive situation. In no way am I encouraging you to stay in a relationship where there is criminal activity, physical abuse, drug abuse, habitual adultery, or pornography forced upon children or spouse.

When I say, "Resolve to stay," I am talking about the relatively trivial issues that are blamed for most divorces today. Too many couples I meet use wimpy reasons to try to justify divorce: "We've just grown apart"; "We don't see eye to eye anymore"; "We've lost that lovin' feeling"; "We can't get past our financial issues." Those are not reasons for divorce.

Not everything needs to be a major battle, so I counsel you to choose your battles carefully. Pet peeves and annoying personality quirks are best left alone and should definitely not be harped on. Also, choose your words carefully. Don't ever use the D-word even as part of a punch line for a joke. Don't tease your mate with words like "my next spouse" or "trading up" or anything of the sort. And choose your audience carefully. Live out your commitment to each other and to the marriage in front of your children. They need the security, especially if they have ever felt or heard the threat of divorce.

Submit to the Authority of Your Church

I beg you, if you haven't already, plug into a solid local church on the day you return from your honeymoon. Join a small group or Sunday school class where you can be in fellowship with other believers. Give those in the community the freedom to speak into your lives. Your young marriage is counting on it. Submit to the leaders of your church and respect their authority. Don't bolt when they say or do something you don't like, because you need them to point out sin in your life. Sometimes they will need to point out sin that is obvious. Other times they will need to point out sin that is leading you down an even more destructive path: "The sins of some men are obvious, reaching the place of judgment ahead of them; the sins of others trail behind them" (1 Tim. 5:24).

When your sin is blatant and flagrant, good leaders will call you on it. Be a young groom or young bride who listens when rebuked. We all need accountability, and the church is there to help us be men and women of God. Follow their leadership by obeying: "Obey your leaders and submit to their authority. They keep watch over you as men who must give an account. Obey them so that their work will be a joy, not a burden, for that would be of no advantage to you" (Heb. 13:17).

A church wedding is only the start; it's even better to have a church marriage. For almost fifteen years now, Amy and I have been leaning on the support of our church family and the older men and women in our congregation. Don't be afraid to ask for help when you need it.

Check out www.youngandinlove.com for video podcasts, articles, and resources to help you prepare for marriage.

Young and in Love Marriage Journal

When you are married, how will your marriage struggles build your character?

What struggles and pain have you already had to work through in your relationship?

What will it take to keep you from trying to change your spouse?

Make a list of the character issues that you need to work on.

Do you have a church? Are you plugged in? Will you submit to the authority of the church? Will you go to leaders of the church for help?

Fox Alert: Trials

Your young marriage will face hardships, and you must choose whether you will allow those hardships to be foxes. As you open your heart to God, you will see how all hardships have "spiritual gems." Treasure hunt for the gems and learn from each trial you face together. Paul said that suffering produces character (Rom. 5:3–4), and James told us to "consider it pure joy, my brothers, whenever you face trials of many kinds, because you know that the testing of your faith develops perseverance. Perseverance must finish its work so that you may be mature and complete, not lacking anything" (James 1:2–4). Trials are not intended to destroy the Christian; instead, God uses them to make us more like Jesus.

Chapter 13

Eat, Drink, and Be Married

Enjoy life with your wife, whom you love, all
the days of this meaningless life
that God has given you under the sun—all your meaningless days.
For this is your lot in life and in your toilsome labor under the sun.

—Ecclesiastes 9:9

Life is hard, you die, and then you're forgotten. This is the outline of the book of Ecclesiastes. You can see why people avoid this book—it's too depressing! But if you mine the nuggets, you will begin to see God's heart for your life and marriage.

Most people would point to Ephesians 5 as the primary marriage text of the Bible. But to do so overlooks a major marriage nugget in the Old Testament. I get that we are to lay down our lives for our wives, guys, but I think God never intended for us to choose between our life and our wife. Solomon said that we can and should enjoy both.

Life is a grind. In Ecclesiastes 1, word pictures from creation are used to explain our life on this planet. The earth is described as a grinder:

> The words of the Teacher, son of David, king in
> Jerusalem:
>
> "Meaningless! Meaningless!"
>   says the Teacher.
> "Utterly meaningless!
>   Everything is meaningless."
>
> What does man gain from all his labor
>   at which he toils under the sun?
> Generations come and generations go,
>   but the earth remains forever.
> The sun rises and the sun sets,
>   and hurries back to where it rises.
> The wind blows to the south
>   and turns to the north;
> round and round it goes,
>   ever returning on its course.
> All streams flow into the sea,
>   yet the sea is never full.
> To the place the streams come from,
>   there they return again. (vv. 1–7)

We are born into this grinder, and the churning begins. We face hard times and challenges all through life. In your young marriage

you will understand the grind soon enough. You'll probably experience the grind the most in trying to make a living. It may get very
hard. You'll feel the grind when your career pursuits don't go as
planned or when you try to pay bills with an already stretched bank
account. Keep in mind that God already knows about the grind:

> To Adam he said, "Because you listened to your wife
>   and ate from the tree about which I commanded
>   you, 'You must not eat of it,'
>
> "Cursed is the ground because of you;
>   through painful toil you will eat of it
>   all the days of your life.
> It will produce thorns and thistles for you,
>   and you will eat the plants of the field.
> By the sweat of your brow
>   you will eat your food
> until you return to the ground,
>   since from it you were taken;
> for dust you are
>   and to dust you will return." (Gen. 3:17–19)

God gave Adam work to do before sin entered the picture, but
hard, grinding work is now part of the equation as a result of Adam's
disobedience. Be careful not to take the grind out on your spouse.

Don't give up on the text. We need to go a little further through
this tunnel before we start seeing daylight. How long will the grind
last? The Bible says all the way up until the end:

The length of our days is seventy years—
    or eighty, if we have the strength;
yet their span is but trouble and sorrow,
    for they quickly pass, and we fly away. (Ps. 90:10)

Age will not get you out of the grind. Even if you make it to eighty years of age, your life will be tough. "Trouble and sorrow" in this text means gruesome, difficult, and painful, and it's a myth to think that the more years you get under your belt the easier the grind will get. Money cannot buy your way out of it. Degrees cannot outsmart it. Age and maturity won't deliver you from pain and trials.

Solomon actually says the grinder will eventually take over your body. I love to read Ecclesiastes 12 to Amy at night to help us both picture our senior years on the front porch, rocking away:

Remember your Creator
    in the days of your youth,
before the days of trouble come
    and the years approach when you will say,
    "I find no pleasure in them"—
before the sun and the light
    and the moon and the stars grow dark,
    and the clouds return after the rain;
when the keepers of the house tremble,
    and the strong men stoop,
when the grinders cease because they are few,
    and those looking through the windows grow dim;

> when the doors to the street are closed
>> and the sound of grinding fades;
> when men rise up at the sound of birds,
>> but all their songs grow faint;
> when men are afraid of heights
>> and of dangers in the streets;
> when the almond tree blossoms
>> and the grasshopper drags himself along
>> and desire no longer is stirred.
> Then man goes to his eternal home
>> and mourners go about the streets. (vv. 1–5)

You're in the grind all the way to the end, and your only way out of the grind is death. Are you encouraged yet? Life is hard, and then you die. Why in the world are you still reading this chapter?

We'll become fragile, and our bodies will start breaking down. We'll lose our teeth. Our glasses will get thicker and thicker as we begin to lose our eyesight. We will stay inside the house, and the sounds of the marketplace will grow faint to us. We'll nap all day long and wake up every morning at 3:00 a.m. Walking will be difficult for fear of stumbling. Your almond tree will blossom, which means your hair will turn gray. At thirty-six, I am already experiencing this. Then right before death, sex will become difficult if not impossible. The grasshopper starts dragging. Sexual desire is no longer stirred.

I love asking my wife this question: "Amy, will you still love me when my grasshopper's dragging?" And do you know what my wife says? I kid you not, she says, "I think I'll be all right." She then asks me, "What are you going to do, Ted, when your grasshopper starts dragging?" I reply, "The Lord can take me home. Life will just be over." You laugh, but that's what the Bible says: "The grasshopper drags himself along and desire no longer is stirred. Then man goes to his eternal home and mourners go about the streets" (v. 5). Once the desire for sex is gone, man is ready to go be with Jesus.

Here's our recap: Life is a grind, you grow old, stop having sex, and then go to be with Jesus. There is only one more hard part of the outline. Once we die, we will be forgotten:

> Anyone who is among the living has hope—even a live
>   dog is better off than a dead lion!
>
> For the living know that they will die,
>   but the dead know nothing;
> they have no further reward,
>   and even the memory of them is forgotten.
> Their love, their hate
>   and their jealousy have long since vanished;
> never again will they have a part
>   in anything that happens under the sun. (Eccl.
>   9:4–6)

Back in the day, the lion was an esteemed beast, and the dog was a dirty street dweller. Solomon was saying here that your pulse still gives you a shot at life. The celebrity, the rock star, and the billionaire philanthropist will one day be forgotten. We walk into libraries, dining halls, and dormitories with names hanging above the door. Most of us walk underneath those names thousands of times with no clue who those people were or what they did to get a building named after them. It is proof that we will all be forgotten and only that which we do for Christ will last.

When you die, they'll put you in a box, pack your stuff away, eat a little potato salad at a luncheon in your honor, and move on with life. What the heck does all of this have to do with marriage? We're getting there. *Hang on.*

So what do we do in the midst of this grind with the knowledge that we will one day die and be forgotten? What do we do in the midst of trying to make that mortgage payment, of deciding if we should make a career change or seek a promotion? Solomon tells us, "You're not dead yet." So you still have a shot at life.

Let's turn the corner. In the midst of the grind, God still wants you to enjoy your life:

> Go, eat your food with gladness, and drink your wine with a joyful heart, for it is now that God favors what you do. Always be clothed in white, and always anoint your head with oil. (Eccl. 9:7–8)

You and I have a responsibility in the daily grind. Dare I say that part of your purpose in life is to play and have fun? Yes! You are called to enjoy life! In the midst of the grind that is life, while you're still alive, go and do something. Live life and enjoy it! You need to find and hold on to those moments—sharing a meal, laughing, and being joyful. Don't throw that out the window because life is difficult. We can do nothing to escape the grind. So in the meantime, choose joy. And for goodness' sake, do not pretend that your spouse is the grinder.

God did not give me my spouse as part of the grind; rather Amy and I are going through the grinder together. In the same way, you do not have to choose between life and a spouse. You can enjoy life with your spouse in the midst of the grind:

> Enjoy life with your wife, whom you love, all the
> days of this meaningless life that God has given you
> under the sun—all your meaningless days. For this
> is your lot in life and in your toilsome labor under
> the sun. (Eccl. 9:9)

This is the only place in the Bible where it says, "Enjoy life with your wife." You and I do not need to choose between the two, and one does not trump the other. You can have both because marriage enhances life.

I love hearing guys tell me, "I had all sorts of plans, dreams, and goals for the future, but then I got married," or "My wife and I had all sorts of plans, dreams, and goals for the future, but then we had kids." Let me give you the Hebrew term for those statements: "hogwash"! Your spouse was not brought into your life to kill your fun, play, dreams, and goals. And your kids were not brought into your life to be killjoys either.

The grind will have its seasons. According to Dictionary.com, a season is defined as "one of the four periods of the year (spring, summer, autumn, and winter); a period of the year characterized by particular conditions of weather, temperature, etc." God created the Earth on a 23.5 degree axis and placed it in perfect rotation around the sun—hence the seasons. Here in Branson, Missouri, we experience all four seasons, though in some more extreme climates, they may experience only two: dry and rainy. Whatever the case, seasons do not last forever, and the Earth is always refreshed by new conditions.

Enjoying life and marriage is only possible when you grasp the concept of seasons because you will experience many seasons in your life and in your marriage. According to Song of Songs, your young budding love is now in the season of spring:

> See! The winter is past;
>> the rains are over and gone.
> Flowers appear on the earth;
>> the season of singing has come,
> the cooing of doves
>> is heard in our land.
> The fig tree forms its early fruit;
>> the blossoming vines spread their fragrance.
> Arise, come, my darling;
>> my beautiful one, come with me. (2:11–13)

Dating and engagement is a season of delay. Even though Amy and I were engaged through the summer months, I understand what the Shullamite bride-to-be was saying in this passage. The season of delay felt like winter to her. The bud turning to a blossom was springtime and marked their wedding day.

We've had a lot of different seasons in our marriage. The newborn and toddler seasons were tough, but they quickly turned to springtime. The seminary season was a tough season financially, but it, too, turned to spring once I graduated and earned a bit more.

My first few years as a senior pastor was the toughest season of our marriage, but we stuck it out and have enjoyed many springs since. Seasons create a pace and rhythm that breathe hope into a marriage. Thank You, Father, for seasons!

There's a season your marriage needs to be refreshed with regularly. It is the season of laughter:

> There is a time for everything,
>   and a season for every activity under heaven:
>
> a time to be born and a time to die,
> a time to plant and a time to uproot,
> a time to kill and a time to heal,
> a time to tear down and a time to build,
> a time to weep and a time to laugh,
> a time to mourn and a time to dance. (Eccl. 3:1–4)

Laugh in the midst of the grind and remember not to take yourself too seriously. Proverbs 17:22 says, "A cheerful heart is good medicine." Your marriage needs several good doses of this medicine stored in the medicine cabinet. Preacher Henry Ward Beecher once said, "A person without a sense of humor is like a wagon without springs—jolted by every pebble in the road. Humor makes all things tolerable."

Thank You, Lord, for giving us the gift of laughter. If we start laughing more, maybe we can solve the nation's health-care crisis.

You are in a great season right now, but it won't last forever. You will need to discipline your young marriage and be sure to include many times of play, laughter, and pure enjoyment!

Check out www.youngandinlove.com for video podcasts, articles, and resources to help you prepare for marriage.

Young and in Love Marriage Journal

What will be the greatest challenges your young marriage will face?

How will you keep from treating your spouse as the grinder?

List a few of the activities you and your significant other or fiancé(e) enjoy.

What will it take to keep those activities from growing old or boring?

In what areas of your relationship do you need to lighten up?

Fox Alert: The Grind

Catch yourself when you start looking at your spouse as part of the grind. You know you have made him or her a part of the grind when his or her words start sounding like something coming from Charlie

Brown's teacher: "Womp-womp, *womp-womp,* womp-womp." Enjoy life and marriage. Go through the grinder *together* as teammates, not as opponents.

Notes

Chapter 1: Chase the Foxes

1. Shannon Fox and Celeste Liversidge, *Last One Down the Aisle Wins* (New York: St. Martin's Griffin, 2010), 1.

Chapter 2: Please, No More Purity Talks!

1. Mark Regnerus, "The Case for Early Marriage," *Christianity Today*, July 31, 2009, www.christianitytoday.com/ct/2009/august/16.22.html.

2. Ibid.

Chapter 3: The Tone

1. Larry David, "The Engagement," Seinfeld, season 7, episode 1, directed by Andy Ackerman, aired September 21, 1995 (New York: National Broadcasting Company, 2006), DVD.

2. Sheila Marikar, "Jennifer Aniston vs. Bill O'Reilly: The Family Factor," *ABCNews.com*, August 12, 2010, www.abcnews.go.com/Entertainment/jennifer-aniston-bill-oreilly-family-factor/story?id=11383536.

3. Claudia Puig, "'Eat Pray Love'? More like 'Me Me Me amid beautiful scenery,'" *USA Today*, August 12, 2010.

Chapter 4: The Consequences

1. "Median Age at First Marriage, 1890–2007," Information Please® Database, © 2009 Pearson Education, Inc., http://www.infoplease.com/ipa/A0005061.html#ixzz1DO3zuKTO.

2. Mark Gungor, "A Case for Young Marriage," *Young Marriages,* www.youngmarriages. com/articles/34-a-case-for-young-marriage (accessed Feb 2011).

3. Danielle Crittenden, *What Our Mothers Didn't Tell Us* (New York: Simon and Schuster, 1999), 60–61.

4. Ibid., 69.

5. Ibid., 65–66.

6. Gail Saltz, "Are Young Marriages Doomed to Fail?" *iVillage.com,* www.gailsaltz .ivillage.com/love/archives/2006/11/are-young-marriages-doomed-to.html (accessed June 2010).

7. Mark Regnerus, "The Case for Early Marriage," *Christianity Today,* July 31, 2009, www.christianitytoday.com/ct/2009/august/16.22.html.

8. Mark Driscoll, *Religion Saves* (Wheaton, IL: Crossway, 2009), 186.

9. Jessica Bennett and Jesse Ellison, "I Don't: The Case Against Marriage," *Newsweek,* June 11, 2010, www.newsweek.com/2010/06/11/i-don-t.html.

10. Albert Mohler, "The Case Against Marriage, Courtesy of Newsweek," *AlbertMohler. com,* June 25, 2010, www.albertmohler.com/2010/06/25/the-case-against-marriage-courtesy-of-newsweek.

11. Belinda Luscombe, "Who Needs Marriage?", *Time,* November 18, 2010.

Chapter 6: Unnecessary Delays

1. Mark Regnerus, "The Case for Early Marriage," *Christianity Today,* July 31, 2009, www.christianitytoday.com/ct/2009/august/16.22.html.

2. Po Bronson and Ashley Merryman, "Has Being Married Gone Out of Style?", *Time,* Wednesday, Oct. 18, 2006, www.time.com/time/nation/article/0,8599,1547431,00.html.

3. Jeannette J. Lee, "Todd Palin Unique Among Nation's Five First Spouses," *Anchorage Daily News,* May 27, 2007, adn.com.

4. Mike and Harriett McManus, *Living Together: Myths, Risks, and Answers* (New York: Howard Books, 2008), 63–67.

5. Gary Thomas, "Marry Sooner Rather Than Later," *Boundless,* March 13, 2009, www.boundless.org/2005/articles/a0001992.cfm.

6. Gail Saltz, "Are Young Marriages Doomed to Fail?" *iVillage.com,* www.gailsaltz.ivillage .com/love/archives/2006/11/are-young-marriages-doomed-to.html (accessed June 2010).

7. Americans for Divorce Reform, "Correlation of Divorce Rates with Other Factors," *Divorce Reform Page,* http://www.divorcereform.org/cor.html#anchor2349971.

8. Dr. Chuck Stecker, *Men of Honor, Women of Virtue* (Denver: Seismic, 2010), 61.

Chapter 7: Age, Privilege, and Responsibility

1. Sharon Jayson, "It's time to grow up—later," *USA Today,* September 30, 2004, www.usatoday.com/life/lifestyle/2004-09-30-extended-adolescence_x.htm.

2. Ibid.

Chapter 8: Character

1. Charles R. Swindoll, "A Battle for Integrity," *Insights,* March 2003, 1–2.

2. Sharon Jayson, "Divorce threat persists throughout marriage," *USA Today,* September 19, 2007, http://www.usatoday.com/news/health/2007-09-19-divorce-census_N.htm.

3. Mark Driscoll, "The world is filled with boys who can shave," *Washington Post,* August 22, 2010, http://onfaith.washingtonpost.com/onfaith/panelists/mark_driscoll/2010/08/the_world_is_filled_with_boys_who_can_shave.html.

Chapter 9: Chemistry

1. Adapted from the four personality animal types of the lion, otter, golden retriever, and beaver in Gary Smalley and John Trent, PhD, *The Two Sides of Love* (Carol Stream, IL: Tyndale, 1999).

Chapter 11: Calling

1. *The Word in Life Study Bible: New Testament Edition* (Nashville: Thomas Nelson, 1993), 180.

Chapter 12: First Signs of Trouble

1. Tiffany Sharples, "For Worse, Then for Better: Why Facing Stressful Life Events Early in Coupledom Can Lead to Longevity," *Time,* August 8, 2009.

2. Ibid.

3. Ibid.

Scripture Index

1 Timothy 6:6–8

Psalm 37:21

Ephesians 2:10

Genesis 3:5

Genesis 2:24

Chapter 7

1 Timothy 4:12

1 Timothy 4:10

1 Timothy 4:15

1 Timothy 4:16

1 Timothy 5:1

Ecclesiastes 12:1

James 1:2–4

Romans 5:3–5

Genesis 2:24

Ephesians 6:4

Proverbs 23:22–25

Chapter 8

Ephesians 5:1

Psalm 78:72

Song of Songs 2:3

Malachi 2:14

1 Timothy 3:12

1 Timothy 5:8

1 Timothy 2:8

Ephesians 6:4

Deuteronomy 6:6–7

1 Timothy 5:9–14

Matthew 15:8

Proverbs 27:15–16

1 Timothy 2:9–10

Proverbs 31

Ephesians 5:1

Ephesians 5:2

Romans 12:1

Ephesians 5:3

1 Timothy 5:1–2

Matthew 6:24

Ephesians 5:4

James 3:2–6

Ephesians 5:7

1 Timothy 4:12

Song of Songs 3:6

Chapter 9

Song of Songs 2:14

1 Corinthians 7:12–14

1 Peter 3:1–6

Psalm 139:13–16

Romans 15:7

Ephesians 4:2

Chapter 10

Exodus 31:3

Acts 18:2–4

Colossians 3:23

Chapter 11

Ephesians 1:18–19

Ephesians 1:18

Ephesians 2:10

Romans 11:29

2 Thessalonians 2:14

1 Corinthians 1:7–9

1 Peter 2:5, 9

1 Peter 2:19–21

1 Corinthians 7:15–24

Philippians 3:13—4:1

Ecclesiastes 4:12

Chapter 12

Ecclesiastes 7:3

Job 2:9–10

2 Corinthians 12:9

Colossians 3:2

1 Timothy 5:24

Hebrews 13:17

Romans 5:3–4

James 1:2–4

Chapter 13

Ecclesiastes 9:9

Ephesians 5

Ecclesiastes 1:1–7

Genesis 3:17–19

Psalm 90:10

Ecclesiastes 12:1–5

Ecclesiastes 9:4–6

Ecclesiastes 9:7–8

Ecclesiastes 9:9

Song of Songs 2:11–13

Ecclesiastes 3:1–4

Proverbs 17:22